D1187559

COGNITIVE-
BEHAVIOURAL
COUNSELLING
IN *Action*

COUNSELLING
· IN ACTION ·

Series editor: Windy Dryden

Counselling in Action is a series of books developed
especially for counsellors and students of
counselling which provides clear and explicit
guidelines for counselling practice. A special feature
of the series is the emphasis it places on the *process*
of counselling.

Feminist Counselling in Action
Jocelyn Chaplin

Psychodynamic Counselling in Action
Michael Jacobs

Person-Centred Counselling in Action
Dave Mearns and Brian Thorne

Cognitive-Behavioural Counselling in Action
Peter Trower, Andrew Casey and Windy Dryden

COGNITIVE-
BEHAVIOURAL
COUNSELLING
IN

PETER TROWER, ANDREW CASEY
and WINDY DRYDEN

SAGE Publications
London • Newbury Park • Beverly Hills • New Delhi

First published 1988

 SAGE Publications Ltd
28 Banner Street
London EC1Y 8QE

SAGE Publications Inc
2111 West Hillcrest Drive
Newbury Park, California 91320

SAGE Publications Inc
275 South Beverly Drive
Beverly Hills, California 90212

SAGE Publications India Pvt Ltd
32, M-Block Market
Greater Kailash – I
New Delhi 110 048

British Library Cataloguing in Publication data

Trower, Peter, *1938–*
    Cognitive-behavioural counselling in
    action.—(Counselling in action).
    1. Cognitive counselling
    I. Title   II. Casey, Andrew   III. Dryden,
    Windy   IV. Series
    361.3'23

    ISBN 0–8039–8047–7
    ISBN 0–8039–8048–5 Pbk

Library of Congress catalog card number 88–061486

Typeset by Fakenham Photosetting Ltd, Fakenham, Norfolk
Printed in Great Britain by J. W. Arrowsmith Ltd, Bristol

Contents

Preface

This guidebook is designed to contribute towards the practical task of guiding trainee counsellors in the basic skills of cognitive-behavioural counselling (CBC). We have limited ourselves to what we consider to be the basic essentials of the cognitive approach, taking the common elements from the leading schools and adding some of those from other schools where we believe they enhance the effectiveness of a generic CBC approach. However, we have also tried to make the guide self-contained in the sense that we also include some brief guidance on making first contact, establishing rapport, facilitating disclosure and so on. In other words, we have included some other skills that are essential for *any* approach to counselling.

We have tried to make this guidebook as useful as possible to the practitioner. From our own experience, we believe there are four kinds of help that a practitioner will find most useful from such a text on CBC. First, she may want a *brief* outline of the fundamentals of CBC, and some indication of its status in the field. This has been presented in Chapter 1. Second, she may want guidance on CBC presented in the same form as it would be used in practice with a client, with suggested steps to follow and case material to illustrate those steps. This is provided in Part I: A Basic Guide to CBC. The third form of help the practitioner may require is resource material that she can turn to whenever she may need it. We have provided such resource material in Part II. Finally, the fourth form of help required is guidance on particular applications, and so in Part III we give guidance on applications in major emotional problem areas.

In Chapter 1 we provide just enough theory and background to get started, and allow other principles to emerge naturally as they become relevant in counselling in the remainder of the book.

In Part I (Chapters 2, 3 and 4) we provide a basic guide on conducting CBC with an individual client from beginning to end. The section begins with considerations when first receiving a referral, and proceeds step-by-step through the various stages to termination. This section consists of three chapters corresponding to the three stages of CBC: the opening stage of getting started, the middle stage of helping the client to change and to learn the CBC *method* of change, and the closing stage of learning to be independent. This section includes many of the basic skills the counsellor needs, particularly cognitive assessment techniques, and strategies for cognitive intervention. It also includes guidance on establishing therapeutic goals and tasks, structuring homework and overcoming cognitive blocks to change, and setting and maintaining boundary conditions.

Part II (Chapters 5 and 6) is the resources section, containing a broader range of therapeutic techniques than that covered in Part I, and is intended as a supplement to Part I. The two major topics covered are homework setting and methods of disputing and challenging dysfunctional beliefs.

In Part III the book moves from these general CBC skills to specific skills for specific problems, including anxiety (Chapter 7), depression (Chapter 8), and other common emotional problems, namely shame, guilt and anger (Chapter 9). These chapters give guidance on identifying and challenging the particular dysfunctional belief-systems that underpin these emotional problems. These chapters also include sections on some of the classic 'pitfalls' that typically occur.

Three Caveats

Before we start the practical work, there are three important caveats to note about this type of guide. Firstly, it is in no way designed to be (nor could it be) a thorough training in CBC – such a training takes years of theoretical and practical course work, including intensive supervision of counselling work with clients. However, it should serve to help you to interview selected clients from a CBC perspective, to carry out basic cognitive assessments, and formulate and carry out some straightforward treatment strategies.

Secondly, the guide assumes the learner already has basic training in and experience with counselling skills. CBC utilises basic counselling skills extensively and cannot be carried out without such skills.

The last caveat modifies the last two. That is that research shows that untrained lay counsellors often have natural skills at least equal to those who have been trained and practising for many years. Every learner has a repertoire of such skills, many of which quite probably cannot be 'taught' as such, but merely maximised and sharpened. However, some people also have unhelpful skills that are detrimental to clients. The aim of this guide therefore is a modest one – to help people improve, sharpen and deploy their natural positive skills, to give them a powerful theoretical model for organising their skills, and to help them abandon or modify any unhelpful skills. The trainee can use the guide in a self-contained way to achieve these modest goals, but the best use of the guide is in conjunction with a proper supervised course in CBC.

Finally, a word on gender. Throughout the book we have referred to the counsellor as she and the client as he. This is purely a convention to avoid the repetition of he/she or she/he etc. but still reflect the one-to-one nature of a counselling session.

1 An Overview of Cognitive-Behavioural Counselling

When clients seek counselling for emotional problems, they typically describe their problems in terms of their feelings, or in terms of situations with which they cannot cope. The anxious client, for example, may describe how panicky he feels and how hard he finds it to deal with social situations. People rarely come for counselling complaining about their thinking, although their self-defeating thinking is often a major reason for their difficulties.

A common assumption made by many clients, and by people in general, is that other people or unfortunate circumstances are directly responsible for the unpleasant way they feel. For example, one often hears comments such as 'He makes me so angry' or 'She really made me look stupid'. These statements assume that the other person caused the client to feel in the way he did. If this were true, then everyone in a particular situation would experience the same emotions, a fact which is evidently not the case. Take, for example, the case of public speaking. Three speakers may give the same talk which is equally well received by the audience. One speaker may notice the applause and be pleased about the way she performed. The second speaker might feel depressed because he thought that the audience was only clapping to be polite, and that actually they were bored. The third speaker might feel angry because she had put a great deal of effort into preparing the talk and she thought that the audience was not sufficiently appreciative.

It is clear from this example that the same event may lead to a range of emotions depending on how the event is interpreted and evaluated. It is therefore not events that produce bad feelings but the way these events are appraised. This central tenet of cognitive-behavioural counselling (CBC) can be summed up in the now famous words of the philosopher Epictetus in the first century AD: 'Men are disturbed not by things but by the views which they take of them.'

At the heart of CBC lies the idea that our interpretations of our experiences are hypotheses or beliefs rather than facts, and as such may be correct or incorrect to varying degrees. Furthermore, when people hold unrealistic and negative beliefs about themselves or their experiences, an emotional upset will result. If this negative thinking is extreme or persistent, it may lead to an emotional disorder. Depression is likely to result, for example, if a client starts to hold false beliefs such as that his life is totally pointless and that he is worthless.

Thoughts and Beliefs

Two aspects of thinking are particularly relevant to CBC: (a) ordinary fleeting thoughts and images, and (b) underlying beliefs and assumptions which give rise to the thoughts and images.

Thoughts and Images. One of the major figures in CBC, Aaron Beck, gives the name 'automatic thoughts' to thoughts and images occurring involuntarily in the stream of consciousness (Beck, 1976). If these thoughts are negative and unrealistic, an emotional disorder may result. Furthermore, Beck has described how the type of emotional disorder produced will depend upon the content of the thoughts: if a person's thoughts centre around danger or threat, then anxiety may be produced. If loss is the dominant theme of a person's thoughts, depression may result.

Underlying Beliefs. The second major pioneer in CBC, Albert Ellis, emphasises the role of 'irrational beliefs' in emotional disorders (Ellis, 1962). Irrational beliefs are evaluative beliefs such as: 'I should be perfect. If I make a mistake, that proves how useless I am.' Such a belief would be harmful because the client would be extremely upset every time he made a mistake and he might, for example, blame other people in order to avoid admitting a mistake.

Whereas adaptive beliefs are expressed in relative terms which describe the client's preferences, wishes or desires about a situation, irrational beliefs are expressed in extreme terms such as demands, musts, shoulds and oughts. A further defining characteristic of irrational beliefs is that they hinder a person from achieving his or her goals (Ellis, 1977). Take, for example, a client who wants to make friends yet who persistently worries that other people will find him boring. This worry is likely to lead to anxiety in social situations and avoidance of other people, which in turn will hinder the client's achievement of the goal of making friends.

Ellis (1977) identifies three major irrational beliefs: (a) I *must* do well and win people's approval or else I am worthless; (b) other people *must* treat me considerately and kindly in exactly the way I want them to (otherwise, they should be blamed and punished); (c) life *must* give me all that I want, quickly and easily, and give me nothing that I don't want.

Ellis and Bernard (1985) suggest that these kinds of irrational beliefs lead to three common sorts of self-defeating thinking to be found in clients with a range of emotional disorders:

'I am worthless because ...'
'It is awful that ...'
'I can't stand it that ...'

The ABC Model

Ellis (1977) has also put forward an easily remembered model which explains the relationship between thinking and emotions. According to this model, an Activating event A leads to emotional and behavioural Consequences at C, with the emotional consequences being mediated by Beliefs at B. In this book, a model is adopted which is very similar to Ellis's model. The following example will help to clarify the ABC system which we will use, and the use of the ABC system is described in detail in Chapter 2. Suppose a client walks down the road and a work colleague walks by without acknowledging him. As a result he feels depressed. An ABC analysis of this situation might be as follows:

A = activating event   work colleague fails to acknowledge the person

B = beliefs
   (a) inferences   'My colleague has ignored me.'
                       'He must be angry with me.'
                       'He probably dislikes me.'
   (b) evaluation   'It's awful if someone dislikes you.'

C = emotional consequence   depression
    behavioural consequence   future avoidance of colleague

In this example, there may be other, more plausible explanations for the failure of the colleague to acknowledge the client other than the inference drawn by the client. Perhaps the colleague was daydreaming and did not notice the client; perhaps the colleague was in a bad mood and ignores everyone when in this state. Even if the colleague deliberately ignored the client, the conclusion that the colleague does not like the client may be false. Finally, the evaluation that it is awful, that is, catastrophic, if someone does not like you is certainly not true.

Although the activating event for an emotional upset is often an actual incident, equally often it can be a memory, a thought about a future event, or an emotion itself. For example, in clients suffering from panic disorders, panics are often precipitated by fear of fear. The client notices symptoms of his anxiety such as palpitations or breathlessness, and he becomes more afraid because he thinks that things might happen to him such as losing control or passing out, or even having a heart attack and dying.

The above example of the work colleague ignoring the client is also useful to illustrate the self-fulfilling nature of many self-defeating beliefs. If the client believes that his colleague does not like him, he is likely to be cool towards the colleague. The colleague may well detect this coolness, interpret it as unfriendliness, and reciprocate the coolness. The client then interprets the colleague's coolness as confirmatory evidence for his original conclusion that the colleague does not like him. Therefore, when the client jumps to conclusions about the colleague disliking him, he encourages this outcome to occur.

One method, therefore, by which maladaptive thoughts and beliefs create a self-fulfilling prophecy, is by the influence of the client's beliefs on his behaviour. Another way in which a vicious circle is set up is when a client selectively perceives evidence which supports his maladaptive beliefs. It is common, for example, for depressed people to discount positive aspects of situations and to focus on the negative aspects. A depressed client might consider that he had completely messed up a meeting with a friend, because for a few seconds there was an awkward silence.

Cognitive-Behavioural Counselling

There are three main assumptions underlying CBC: (a) that emotions and behaviour are determined by thinking; (b) that emotional disorders result from negative and unrealistic thinking; and (c) that by altering this negative and unrealistic thinking emotional disturbance can be reduced.

Before teaching clients to modify maladaptive thinking, careful preparation is necessary. As Beck's term 'automatic thoughts' implies, maladaptive thinking is often a habit, and clients are usually only semi-aware of its existence. Similarly, some clients are not very aware of the build-up of negative feelings and only become aware of their feelings when they become extremely upset. The first step in CBC is therefore to teach clients to become more aware of thoughts and feelings, and the situations that trigger negative thoughts.

Once a client is able to identify maladaptive thinking, the counsellor needs to help the client to understand the way in which the maladaptive thinking leads to the client's emotional and behavioural problems.

The next step is for the counsellor to check that the client wants to reduce his emotional upset. This may seem obvious, but the need to clarify goals is illustrated by the client who was reluctant to stop appearing anxious at work because he feared that if he looked better his work colleagues would start to put pressure on him again.

The next step in the CBC process is for the counsellor to teach the client how to modify his maladaptive thinking. CBC theory asserts that thoughts and beliefs are hypotheses which can be shown to be true or false by logic or evidence. CBC practice follows directly from the theory and involves helping the client to gather evidence that will disprove unrealistic and self-defeating thinking and thereby change it.

The modification of maladaptive thinking may be achieved by means of a wide range of methods. The counsellor may help the client to dispute the logic of his thinking, by asking, for example, 'How does it follow that you are useless because you have made this mistake?' Alternatively, she may help the client to challenge the evidence for his conclusions by asking, for example, 'What is the evidence that it would be catastrophic if you made a mistake?'

Perhaps the most powerful way of convincing a client to take a different viewpoint is for the client to carry out tasks which test out or contradict his beliefs. We can illustrate this by taking the example cited earlier of the man who felt depressed because a work colleague ignored him. His beliefs were that his colleague disliked him and that this was awful. He could test this out by making friendly approaches to the colleague and observing what response he obtained. If the response was positive, this would help disprove the belief that the colleague disliked him. If the response was consistently negative, he could test his prediction that this would be disastrous by assessing whether the effect *was* actually to ruin his life.

Finally, the client has persistently to challenge negative thinking and persistently to behave in a way that contradicts the negative thinking before he will create a significant shift in the way that he feels and behaves.

The above description gives a flavour of the methods involved in CBC, and these will be described in detail in the remainder of the book. In summary, the steps involved in cognitive-behavioural counselling are to teach the client to:

(a) monitor emotional upsets and activating events;
(b) identify maladaptive thinking and beliefs;
(c) realise the connections between thinking, emotions and behaviour;
(d) test out maladaptive thinking and beliefs by examining the evidence for and against them;
(e) substitute the negative thinking with more realistic thinking.

Misconceptions about CBC

CBC and Behavioural Counselling
A common misconception about CBC is that it is a 'talking' therapy, as opposed to behavioural counselling which is a 'practical' therapy which works by changing behaviour directly. For example, it might be assumed that a client suffering from agoraphobia will simply talk about his fear with a cognitive-behavioural counsellor but actually be taken out and encouraged to face situations by the behavioural counsellor. However, this is a misconception – the difference between the two is simply one of emphasis. The cognitive-behavioural counsellor also employs practical tasks, but she uses such tasks in order to change thinking. Take the case of a woman with agoraphobia who avoids going out to shops and other public places, and experiences severe panic symptoms when she does. The behavioural counsellor 'exposes' her to the feared stimulus on a number of occasions with the aim of 'extinguishing' the fear response. The cognitive-behavioural counsellor does much the same sort of thing, but for quite different reasons. For example, the counsellor finds out that this client is convinced that if she went out shopping more than just a short way from home, something dreadful would happen to her – she would either die or would completely lose control. Since she never goes out, this belief has never been put to the test (understandably, given her belief). The counsellor would, after careful preparation, take her to stay in the shopping area in order for her to discover the truth of an alternative belief, that she will neither fall to pieces nor die but simply have harmless but uncomfortable anxiety symptoms that will fade with time.

It can be seen that behavioural tasks are incorporated into cognitive-behavioural approaches to counselling because behaviour change is a powerful way of modifying beliefs. The most effective way for a depressed client to disprove his belief that he cannot do anything is by actually carrying out specific tasks. Completing these tasks directly contradicts the self-defeating belief.

In this book, the term 'behavioural' refers to the setting of tasks which are carried out in order to dispute self-defeating beliefs. We are not referring to the application of the principles of operant and classical conditioning. Cognitive procedures can be readily and effectively combined with procedures based upon these conditioning theories (see, for example, Kanfer and Goldstein, 1980), but it is beyond the scope of this book to cover this area.

Client–Counsellor Relationship
A second misconception about CBC is that the relationship between

the client and counsellor is considered unimportant. Disturbed relationships are centrally involved in many psychological problems and the client's interpersonal problems are often reflected in the relationship between the client and the counsellor. One client, for example, believed that people were always trying 'to make her look a fool' and she interpreted a mistake over an appointment as evidence that the counsellor was trying to make her look stupid. Exploration of the client's thoughts about the counsellor subsequently proved to be very fruitful.

In CBC, the counsellor attempts to assess interpersonal beliefs, while resisting being drawn into reacting to the client's behaviour. She then attempts to use the information gained from her relationship with the client in order to help the client to change maladaptive interpersonal beliefs. The good cognitive-behavioural counsellor will be skilfully monitoring the therapeutic relationship throughout the course of the counselling.

Positive Thinking
A common initial misunderstanding about CBC is that it is just 'positive thinking'. However, this is not the case, for in CBC the aim is not to teach the client to think positively but to teach him to think realistically. When things go seriously wrong, it would be maladaptive for us to take a wholly positive view of the situation and be pleased by it. What marks out someone with an emotional problem is the severity and duration of that person's distress, and how extreme and global his negative thinking about the situation is. For instance, a breakdown of a relationship may have realistically bad consequences for a person, but a severe depression will only result if the person views the event in extreme and global terms. (For example, 'My life is now in ruins. I can never be happy without her. She should not have treated me this way.') In this case, the counsellor would not try to convince the client that the breakdown of the relationship does not matter, but rather that it is not catastrophic, nor need it have the far-reaching negative effects that the client predicts. It can be a powerful combination for the CBC counsellor to show empathy and understanding of her client's predicament, yet help the client to put what has happened to him into a realistic perspective.

Importance Given to Childhood Relationships
A major difference between CBC and psychodynamic therapies lies in the degree of importance given to exploring early childhood experiences for the origins of maladaptive patterns of thinking and behaviour. In CBC it can be helpful to explore early experiences to enable the client to place his problems in a historical context, but this

is not seen as a major part of the counselling. The CBC view is that people are not disturbed so much by past events as by the way that these events are viewed in the present. Take, for example, the case of a depressed person who believes that she is worthless. Her depression is not produced by a childhood experience such as her mother telling her that she was useless, but by the fact that she continues to think and believe this.

Skills Training Model
One further feature of CBC worth mentioning at this stage is that CBC is based upon a skills training model. The aim of CBC is not to change clients' beliefs for them, but to teach clients the skills necessary for them to identify and modify their own self-defeating thoughts and beliefs. Although the counsellor is active and directive in CBC, the client is expected to be actively engaged in the counselling, and the counselling is viewed as a collaborative endeavour.

Now that the basic model and characteristics of CBC have been outlined, we turn next to a detailed description of the methods of CBC.

PART I   A BASIC GUIDE TO COGNITIVE-BEHAVIOURAL COUNSELLING

Every human encounter has a basic structure. There is an opening, there is a period of interaction with a particular goal or purpose, and there is a closing (Argyle and Trower, 1979). So, for example, we greet someone, we talk about something, and we say farewell. The same structure also applies to entire relationships, in that they start with a first encounter, proceed through an unspecifiable number of interactions and conclude with a separation or termination (Duck and Gilmour, 1981). Despite the vast differences in different types of interaction, they all follow these basic rules (Goffman, 1971). This structure is so basic to social interaction that we barely notice it – whether we are passing a friend in the street, or whether we are conducting counselling – but it is useful, because it helps us to know what to do, even if the other person is a complete stranger. This seems to us, therefore, the least intrusive, and most natural way of structuring our guide to cognitive-behavioural counselling. It will make intuitive sense to both counsellor and client, and will also help the trainee counsellor keep her bearings without constraining her direction or her creativeness.

The triadic structure of opening, interacting and closing can be applied at several levels. It can be applied at the level of the interview – each interview is obviously opened and closed and has a middle section with a particular working theme. It can be applied at the macro level, in that counselling has a beginning stage, a middle stage and a termination stage. Each stage consists of a number of phases, and each phase is introduced, explored and then rounded off or summarised before a new phase is introduced.

Using this triadic model we can think of counselling as a journey with a beginning, a pathway that gradually and somewhat unpredictably unfolds, and an end. When the counsellor first meets a client, she has no idea where the journey will take them, and there is uncertainty, and apprehension for both client and counsellor. But the counsellor can, and does act, as guide, with the help of this three-sequence model. She knows she must start a relationship and help the client begin the journey, to work at making progress along the way, and finally, to bring it to a conclusion – with hope, but with no guarantee of success. She knows within this overall structure that each episode – that is, each interview – also has to be opened, has a theme or part of a project to be worked through and has obstacles which need to be tackled, and has to be ended. The precise content of what she does depends on the 'school' of counselling that she adopts. This book will teach (or rather contribute towards teaching) the cognitive-behavioural 'school'.

The Major CBC Tasks

We can now show how the triadic model aids the counsellor in helping the client in practice. At its simplest, the counsellor has to help the client to get started on the therapeutic journey (Stage 1: Getting Started), teach the client the cognitive-behavioural method of change (Stage 2: Teaching the CB Method of Change), and finally, help the client learn to overcome blocks to change and independence as he prepares for termination (Stage 3: Overcoming Blocks to Change and Independence).

Stage 1: Getting Started
Usually the client is not pursuing his important life goals; he is in some sense 'stuck'. He may be depressed and deeply cynical about doing or becoming anything he wants to do or become, he may be so anxious that he is avoiding his life goals, or he may be so angry he is damaging his own life and that of others. The counsellor's first task is to help her client find a way to get *started* again, and get out of the rut in which he is stuck. This may or may not mean proceeding with this form of counselling or with this counsellor. If the decision is to proceed, then the counsellor stimulates and guides the client to take the first tentative steps. This is stage 1. It may take several interviews, each of which have their openings and closings, and each of which have phases which build into the overall task of the first stage – getting started.

Stage 2: Teaching the CB Method of Change
If the counsellor and client conclude in stage one that continuing with CBC is appropriate, then the next stage is to teach the CB method of change. The counsellor's task is twofold: not only to engage the client in the process of change directly – the counsellor's customary role – but also, and just as importantly, to teach the client the *theory and method* of change itself. The philosophy of CBC is that the client is taught how to understand and overcome his problems, rather than simply receive 'treatment' like a prescription. This facilitates the

client taking a major role in the process of change, and starts the preparation for independence and termination in stage 3. Stage 2 occupies the middle interviews.

Stage 3: Overcoming Blocks to Change and Independence
The last stage in CBC is to help the client to learn to use CBC to solve problems independently of the counsellor, and so prepare for termination. The intention of CBC so far has been to help the client to change *and* learn the CBC method of change. Now the counsellor builds on this growing independence by focusing on helping the client solve the problems that arise as he learns to take the initiative in using CBC. The aim is to make the counsellor largely redundant, and the client independent.

The Structure of Part I

A chapter of the guide is devoted to each of these three stages of counselling. Each chapter begins with a summary of the aims and contents of that stage. The remainder of the chapter is then divided up into the three phases. Each phase in turn consists of a number of tasks with their accompanying skills, arranged as follows:

1 A description in general terms of a task and a skill or series of skills.
2 An action summary which describes in more specific terms an optional series of numbered steps designed to implement (1).
3 A case example which illustrates one way of using the action summary. The numbered steps in the case example correspond to the numbered steps in the action summary. We don't always give an example for all the steps as this would make the case examples too long and cumbersome, but the steps illustrated should be clear from the numbering.

In order to make the guide as realistic as possible, we base the case examples on one client, whom we take from initial referral right through all stages to termination. Our client – Andrew Smith (a fictitious person) – is first introduced in Chapter 2, at the beginning of his counselling. We say goodbye to him at the end of Chapter 4.

2   Stage 1: Getting Started

The main aim of stage 1 is to try to help the client move from a position where he is immobilised by his difficulties to a point where he begins to experience some change. This entails establishing a working relationship with the client, establishing a preliminary, shared understanding of the problem, and starting a course of action that will begin a process of change.

We outline below a series of tasks and provide a time frame of three 'phases' to help the counsellor decide on the sequence and timing of these tasks.

Opening Phase

Induction
This outlines the steps from preparation before meeting the client, through the initial greeting and introductory remarks, up to exploration of the problem. This includes an open exchange of information and views about what can realistically be expected from CBC.

Exploration
This is when the counsellor encourages the client to talk about his difficulties in an open-ended way, using basic counselling skills.

Middle Phase

Initial Cognitive Assessment
This is when the counsellor carries out her first analysis of the thoughts and beliefs underlying specific problems mentioned in the exploration phase.

Initial Cognitive Intervention
This is when the counsellor helps the client to learn more helpful and more realistic alternative ways of thinking, leading to better ways of reacting emotionally and behaviourally to events.

Closing Phase

Homework
This is when client and counsellor negotiate tasks that the client agrees to carry out outside the counselling session, during which the client will use his alternative way of thinking.

Boundary Conditions
This is when client and counsellor agree on the ground rules for the future counselling sessions.

Which steps are essential? As we go through the phases and tasks below, we will make it clear that some tasks are better carried out in a specific phase, but for others the placement is optional.

How long should stage 1 take? Stage 1 begins, of course, with the initial interview, and it is optional how many further interviews are needed to complete it, as we shall see. However, stage 1 should not take *too* long, because it is important that the client starts working on his problem fairly early, not only to bring some relief to his immediate distress but also to stimulate and maintain his motivation.

OPENING PHASE

How is the CB counsellor to know how to begin? What necessary steps might there be? These thoughts often lead the novice to such a guide as this, in the hope of finding out 'how to do it'. The best place, however, for the trainee counsellor to look is, first, the client, and second, herself. Even at this early stage she can follow some tentative hunches: the client is likely to be unhappy and demoralised, believing himself helpless to find a solution to his difficulties, wanting help and yet hating to ask, pessimistic about anyone being able to help, even if he does ask. The client will have ruminated for months, perhaps years about his difficulties, and will have many ideas about the problem but will still be profoundly confused, ending up in ever more vicious circles of negative thinking. He will also have some vague – or even clear – notions about what will help him – perhaps about what kind of 'treatment' or what kind of 'doctor'. He will expect to be asked – and will usually want to talk – about his difficulties, but may find it very difficult, embarrassing, even harrowing, to do so. He may want the counsellor to be an expert, who will treat him with respect, give him time to tell his story, and to understand. Yet he may expect the counsellor to be too busy with more 'important' things, and to judge his problem as trivial and the interview as a waste of time.

These are important issues, since it is at this early stage of CBC that the counsellor is most likely to lose her client. For this – and other – reasons, the opening phase consists of the two main tasks of induction and exploration.

Induction and Interview Openings

Preparation before Seeing the Client
Sometimes the counsellor will have no knowledge of the client at all, and be in no position to make any pre-interview preparation. In such cases the counsellor has to begin the preparation at the first interview, described below. However, in many other cases the counsellor does have, or can acquire, information about the client. In such cases the counsellor has the option of briefing herself on the client before the first interview. Opinions vary as to how much case material the counsellor should read before seeing the client. One opinion is that as much information as possible on the client's diagnosis, symptoms and history should be obtained, so that the counsellor can make the most efficient use of time, reduce preliminary questioning, and so on. Another opinion is that some of this information, especially from other professionals, such as previous diagnoses, will prejudice the counsellor and make it more difficult for her to be totally open and client-centred – an important point for the CB counsellor, who has to deal with the client's way of thinking. Our own recommendation is two-fold: first, send or give the client a simple biographical data sheet which, in addition to the usual basic information on the client, his family and his educational and occupational background, asks for the main and subsidiary problems and their onset, factors which might have a bearing on the problems (for example, relationships), any kind of previous or present help, medication etc., and any additional information the client might think relevant. Secondly, the counsellor should confine herself to reading only this information, because it originates from the client, and the referral letter, if any. Other case material is often best left until after the first interview.

It can be useful to prepare the client for what to expect in CBC. This can be done prior to the first interview, either by sending the client a brief handout on CBC and an idea of recommended client and counsellor roles, or by a more elaborate induction procedure, with videotape demonstrations of CBC and productive client behaviours. However, such client induction can also be carried out during the opening interviews, as we shall see.

The Initial Interview
At this first face-to-face contact with the client, the counsellor has to concern herself with the most facilitative way of beginning a special

kind of relationship. The counsellor has to open the channels of communication with the client which initially may well be closed. We will focus on two aspects of this. The first is concerned with counsellor 'qualities', the second with client 'attitudes'. First, we suggest three initial counsellor qualities or skills which will help the client to open up to the counsellor.

Confidence. It is best if the counsellor is reasonably knowledgeable about CBC, and is seen as such by the client, who will want to be assured that the counsellor has the expertise to help him. A relaxed manner will contribute to an impression of confidence.

Unconditional positive regard. It is important that the counsellor values the client as a person, and that she communicates this to the client. She should also show that this positive regard is unconditional. One of the main aims of CBC will be to teach the client to adopt this unconditional regard towards himself. The counsellor can communicate this quality by offering, for example, a warm greeting (see below), maintaining good eye contact, leaning slightly forward, giving minimal listening responses like nods and 'mm's', by clarifying and asking questions, by paraphrasing, and by being committed to understanding what the client is saying.

Empathic understanding. It is equally important that the counsellor understands the client and his way of thinking, and is experienced as understanding *by* the client. The basic empathy skill is reflection of feeling, but other basic counselling skills are also important.

This is by no means an exhaustive list of counsellor 'qualities'. We will introduce others as they become relevant.

Second, the client may have unhelpful attitudes which may block him from communicating openly with the counsellor. For example, he may have perceptions and expectations of CBC and the person of the counsellor, as well as of himself, which could, if left unexplored, interfere with or even destroy the counselling process, but which could, if revealed, give clues about the client's way of thinking about himself and others in his life. These clues may be invaluable later in CBC assessment and intervention. Here are some of the possibilities.

Perception of the counsellor. The counsellor is perceived as too busy, too important, and has other more important things to do, or the counsellor is too junior (not important enough). The counsellor is seen as wishing to punish the client (for being 'bad' perhaps), or at the other extreme, the counsellor will save the client and solve all the client's problems.

Perception of himself as client. A common self-perception is that the client is unworthy of the counsellor's help and attention, and so she will spend little time with him and soon pass him on to a more junior person. A client may think his problems too trivial to bother the counsellor with, or so serious that there is no cure, and for this reason will be wasting the counsellor's time. Two not uncommon extremes are that he sees himself as a victim of a vindictive world, and has to be vigilant and on the defensive for fear of attack, versus seeing himself as a helpless weakling who needs to be helped by strong saviours. Such self-perceptions clearly fit in with some of the other-perceptions described above. The counsellor needs to be aware of how the client relates to her, in order to (a) resist being drawn into the offered role, and (b) be in a position to use this information in assessing the client's self-concept.

The rationale for the referral. Two extremes in this case are that (a) the GP, for example, has referred the client to a specialist for a cure, versus (b) the GP has just 'passed the buck' to the counsellor and the counsellor will pass it to someone else.

The nature of counselling itself. Will it be an instant cure, or a waste of time? In other words, does the client have unrealistic evaluations and predictions, or preconceived notions about what he needs and what will work?

Why does the counsellor seek this kind of information about the client? Many of the perceptions we have discussed stem from the client's poor self-concept, and the beliefs underlying those perceptions will be the focus of assessment and intervention. Also, as we shall emphasise throughout this guide, the effective CB counsellor remains constantly alert and responsive to her client, and seeks to understand her client's thoughts, feelings and disposition, so that she can respond in appropriate therapeutic ways. This 'reaching for understanding' is very much the focus of the exploration phase, which follows later.

Action Summary

In order to make 'concrete' these general points about induction of the client and interview openings, we suggest the following steps as a tentative guide for the first and second interviews.

1 Brief yourself on the client (before actually meeting him) from his biographical data sheet and any referral letter. Make a judgment as to whether it will be appropriate to be on Christian name terms with your client. This choice depends both on the client's and your preferences about the relative formality/informality of the relationship.

2 Be reasonably 'conventional' in dress and manner, to avoid stimulating any client attitudes which may interfere with rapport-building.

3 Greet the client warmly and firmly, and by name.

4 Introduce yourself briefly, giving your name and professional status.
5 Say who referred him and ask if he has any thoughts about the referral.
6 If the client seems agitated, it may help to start by engaging in small talk (for example, his journey to the clinic) and to take down formal details like name, address, telephone number, marital status and occupation.
7 Ask the client what he expects from counselling. If necessary briefly explain the purpose of counselling and how it aims to help solve problems. Use analogies or examples if necessary. If induction material was previously sent to the client, invite him to discuss this. This item (7) can be left to the end of the first interview or the beginning of the second, if it is clear, for example, that the client is pressing to tell his story.
8 Ask the client if he has any anxieties or worries about coming for counselling. Give the client reassurance, or undertake to give him an answer during the course of the interview. This item can also be left to the end or to the second interview.
9 From the second interview, ask the client to report on any events that have happened since the last appointment. This will include any activities or happenings of concern to the client, as well as functioning as a report request for any homework set during the last interview.

Case Example
Before giving our first example, we first introduce our client, Andrew Smith, a fictitious person, though his experiences are drawn from real case material. We follow Andrew through the complete course of CBC in this and the next two chapters.

Andrew Smith was referred by his GP, Dr Adams, for counselling for a problem described as 'an anxiety state with episodes of depression'. Andrew is 22, single, and an only child living at home with his mother and step-father. He has a job as a clerk in an insurance office. His main problem is social anxiety, bordering at times on phobia with near-panic attacks in certain enclosed and crowded places, especially when he has to do something like eating (in a restaurant), drinking (in a pub) or writing (in an office). He has a poor self-concept, and though he has a girlfriend, expects her to give him up. He is becoming increasingly withdrawn, staying at home and doing very little except feeling depressed. He is quiet, and often rather unrewarding company, though he has a couple of good friends, and can share his problems with them. His mother is over-indulgent, his step-father rather despising. Andrew doesn't get on well with either of them, and spends little time in their presence. Andrew sought the help of his GP for 'feelings of sickness' when he went out. The GP thinks it is an anxiety problem, and referred Andrew to a cognitive-behavioural counsellor, Mrs Dorothy Jones. The following dialogue starts with the first meeting and first interview between Andrew and Mrs Jones.

3, 4, 5 *Counsellor*: Hallo, Mr Smith. [*Offers chair.*] Make yourself comfortable. I am Mrs Jones. I am a counsellor, and as you know we are meeting today at the suggestion of your GP, Dr Adams. Before we start I'd like to ask you how you feel about coming here to see me. Feel free to say what you think.

Client: Well, the GP thought you might be able to help me. He didn't say very much.

Counsellor: So that was what your GP thought. What do you think yourself?

Client: Well, I've got to try something.

Counsellor: Yes, OK. Did you have any other thoughts, for example perhaps on the way here?

Client: . . . I felt a bit nervous . . . didn't know what was going to happen . . . may be wasting your time.

8 *Counsellor*: So you had at least two concerns. You were worried about wasting my time and worried about what would happen. First, it is my job to help you deal with your emotional difficulties, just as it is your GP's job to provide you with help with physical illness. Secondly, today we will just talk, and I hope you will tell me all about the difficulties you're having, and if we both think it is right to go on, I'll help you to find ways of solving some of those problems. Of course there is more to it than that, but what do you think so far?

[*The client seems reassured and ready to continue.*]

7 *Counsellor*: One last question before we start properly. I sent you a brief description of what this form of counselling is about. Did you have any thoughts about that?

Client: Only that I am quite happy with it. This was the way I thought it would go.

The counsellor continues to seek the kind of information listed above at the beginning and end of interviews, as well as at relevant points during interviews where the work of counselling might be putting a strain on the therapeutic alliance. One of these points, as we shall see, is when the counsellor puts pressure on the client to carry out uncomfortable homework assignments.

Exploration through Basic Counselling Skills

After eliciting as far as possible the client's expectations and any 'hidden agendas' he may have about counselling, the counsellor moves to the content – getting the client to talk about the difficulties that brought him to seek help. There are various ways of achieving this. The way we recommend in this phase of CBC is by means of an open and unstructured style of exploration.

Why should the counsellor want to adopt this style of interviewing? There are at least four reasons. First, the client is given the opportunity to tell his own story in his own way, and the counsellor is then better able to understand the client's point of view. Secondly, if the client feels better understood, this will help to strengthen the relationship or bond, which in turn means the counsellor will be able to influence the client more. Thirdly, the counsellor will be able to more accurately tailor CBC to the client's needs if she is fully aware of what George Kelly (1955) called the client's 'construct system', that is, his way of understanding himself, his world and his difficulties. Fourthly, this establishes a pattern in which the client will take an active rather than passive role in CBC.

However, this style of interviewing is quite difficult to achieve. The client may have been expecting a medical-type interview consisting of closed-ended, fact- and symptom-seeking questions. Certainly, he will probably be expecting the counsellor to take the initiative in directing the content of the interview, and the counsellor will typically feel under pressure to take this role. However, the counsellor can usually overcome this client expectation by explaining the intention and the reason for open exploration, and facilitating the client by means of basic counselling skills. We are assuming a basic knowledge of counselling skills here, and give some guidance on the use of these skills in the following action summary.

Action Summary
A possible action sequence for exploration is as follows:

1 The counsellor concludes the opening remarks.
2 The counsellor gives the client an open invitation to talk about himself, his world and his difficulties. She explains to the client why she is adopting this style of interviewing and asks if the client is agreeable.
3 In the case of clients who can't get started, or remain off the point, there are various techniques, such as the 'Single word technique' (Lazarus, 1981), in which the client is asked to say what single word he would choose to describe his difficulties, and then to use the word in a sentence. Subsequently, the counsellor resists the temptation to fill silences, but periodically helps the client with exploratory open questions.
4 Once the client starts talking, the counsellor facilitates the client with basic non-selective listening skills like attending behaviour and minimal encouragers to talk.

5 After the client has talked for a short while, the counsellor facilitates the client with selective listening skills, such as open and
closed questions, paraphrases, reflections and summaries.

Case Example

1 *Counsellor*: Right, I think we agree about what we should be doing,
though we will constantly return to look at this and any worries about
counselling you may have as we go along. Perhaps now then you would
like to tell me about the difficulties you've been experiencing. We have
over forty-five minutes so there is plenty of time.
   Client: Well, er, what aspect of it do you want to hear about first?
2 *Counsellor*: That's a good question. If I were a doctor, I would ask you a lot
of questions about symptoms and so on about your illness. But here the
situation is different. You don't have an illness. You've had an emotional upset in your life, and I need to hear your story in your own words,
told in your own way. Perhaps you could start with what led you to go to
see the GP.
   Client: Well it all started one day when I was sitting in a restaurant with a
friend of mine, and started to feel sick and very hot. I couldn't understand what was happening to me. I often feel tensed up but this was
something quite new.
4 *Counsellor*: Mm. [*Pause*] Tell me a bit more about that.

The client goes on with his story; and the counsellor continues to
facilitate this with basic counselling skills.

Moving from Exploration to Assessment

There is no hard and fast rule about when to move from the open,
client-directed exploration phase to the more structured, counsellor-
directed assessment phase. The CB counsellor would come between
the person-centred counsellor, who remains exploratory throughout
counselling, to the radical behaviourist who may well be directive
from the beginning. The counsellor will decide whether to move to
the assessment phase of CBC on the basis of (a) whether she has
enough information to proceed to this phase and (b) whether the
client is ready for the shift of emphasis. She may choose to explore for
the whole of the first interview if the client seems to want to talk
(though the counsellor should ensure the client remains problem-
oriented), or she may explore for half the first interview. Whatever
strategy is chosen, the counsellor is advised to negotiate sensitively
with the client the transition from the first phase to the second. For
example, the counsellor may leave the decision to the client and say:
'You have given me a very good idea in general of the difficulties you
have been facing. Are there any more things you want to talk about
now, or shall we focus on one or two of those specific problems and
get some more details about them first?' Alternatively, the counsel-

lor may steer the client gently in the direction of the assessment phase by first summarising what the client has recently said and then saying: 'Now that you have given me the general picture, shall we focus on one or two of the problems you mentioned?'

MIDDLE PHASE

By this point the client will hopefully have outlined some of his most pressing difficulties in general terms, and the counsellor will have encouraged this free-ranging exploration. But now the counsellor faces the task of getting the client to start work on his problems and to understand how therapeutic change can happen. How does the counsellor achieve this? CBC offers a clear philosophy and *modus operandi* for this task, and this is what we shall outline in this section. It consists of two steps – cognitive assessment, and cognitive intervention. We will be returning to both these steps in more detail in the next stage of CBC.

Initial Cognitive Assessment

Cognitive-Behavioural Theory
Unlike a behavioural approach, which largely confines itself to behaviours and the stimuli that maintain them, the cognitive-behavioural approach is concerned with the whole range of human expression – thought, feeling, as well as behaviour and the array of triggering events in the environment. Without a clear model, the task of assessment would be confusing in the extreme. However, cognitive assessment is structured tightly according to cognitive-behavioural theory. An understanding of this theory is essential to carrying out cognitive assessment and intervention. One way of thinking about it, and remembering it easily, is in terms of the ABC as referred to in Chapter 1, and defined here as follows:

A = Activating event.
B = Beliefs, thoughts etc. about A.
C = Emotional and behavioural Consequences of B.

What this means is that emotional distress and problematic behaviour, C, are the consequences not of events themselves, A, but of negative inferences and evaluations of these events, B. There are four things to note about the nature of Bs.

1 Bs (beliefs) include inferences about what may happen or has happened, and evaluations about how good or bad those various events are. Whatever the type of belief, they all share one thing in

common. Beliefs are mini-theories which may be right or wrong, valid or invalid, depending on whether or not there is evidence for them.

2 However, the client mistakenly regards his Bs not as Bs at all but as facts or events, that is, As, and within this reasoning, not thought to be subject to disproof.

3 Some of the beliefs the client mistakenly regards as facts or events are very negative, and are therefore very distressing for the client.

4 The client, therefore, has an A–C formula, for explaining what is happening to him, in which A, the bad event, directly causes C, the emotional distress. One task of CBC is to persuade the client that it is the bad evaluation B that produces the C.

What the counsellor has to do in cognitive assessment is to identify not only the As and Cs but also to identify the Bs – the 'cause' of the distress. She has to identify the anxious beliefs, or the depressing beliefs, or the angry beliefs, and so on.

To give an example, our client Andrew Smith experiences panic and behaves avoidantly, C, not because – as he thinks – of the crowded cafe, A, but because of his beliefs about the cafe, B, which are, as we shall see, that something bad is going to happen to him.

There are various uses we make of the ABC theory. The first is simply to identify the client's As, Bs and Cs in the initial assessment. Secondly, we use the theory to help us reach a tentative hypothesis, or formulation of the problem. Thirdly, we use the theory to help the client understand the cause of his difficulties. Fourthly, of course, we use it to structure our interventions. We will deal with each in turn.

ABC Assessment
The counsellor uses the theory to guide her in carrying out an initial assessment. From the general picture the client may have so far described, she first focuses on a specific incident, or what Wessler and Wessler (1980) call an emotional episode. Secondly, she uses the theory to systematically obtain information on the event A, the thoughts B, about the event, the consequent feelings and behaviours C and the outcome or effect of those feelings and behaviours. It is useful to follow a procedure such as the following:

1 Assess the C,
2 Assess the A,
3 Connect A and C,
4 Assess B,
5 Connect B to C.

An option is to assess A before C. The important thing to stress is that A and C are generally assessed before B.

Activating event	Beliefs (about A)		Consequences (of B)	
Describe actual or anticipated event 1	List dysfunctional thoughts/images 2	List functional alternative thoughts/images 3	List dysfunctional emotions/behaviours 4	List functional emotions/behaviours 5

Figure 1 *ABC form*

The ABC form. When collecting this information it is useful to write it down in three columns under the headings: Activating Events (real or anticipated), Beliefs (dysfunctional thoughts, images about A), and Consequences (dysfunctional emotional and behavioural consequences of B). This ABC assessment method is widely used in CBC, and an extended ABC Form is given in Figure 1. We recommend carrying out two or three ABC assessments rather than one at this stage, since the counsellor will often find that several emotional episodes have an underlying belief in common, and the counsellor will find it useful to identify the underlying belief in making her formulation – a point we come to in the next section. The whole procedure is described more concretely in the following action summary and the case example.

Action Summary

1 Ask the client for an example of one of the problems he had been talking about during the exploration phase.

2 Ask, 'How did you feel in that situation?' or reflect the feeling if given. It is essential to get a strong, dysfunctional feeling – for example, panic, not just apprehension – otherwise the counsellor will not be able to get at the client's dysfunctional thinking.

3 Write down the client's answer in the dysfunctional C column of the ABC form. Show the client what you are writing, and explain the three columns, though you need not, at this stage, explain the meaning of the ABCs – that will come later.

4 Ask, 'What happened?' or 'What led up to that?' or paraphrase the Activating event if given.

5 Write down the client's description in the A column. Show the client as you write.

6 Summarise briefly: 'You say you felt . . . [C] because . . . [A]' or 'You say . . . [A] made you feel . . . [C]'. (Use the client's own words, and show him the words on the form at the same time.)

7 Ask, 'What thoughts about . . . [A] were going through your head at the time?' Or if the client cannot easily produce his thoughts ask, 'Why did you feel so . . . [C] about . . . [A]?' or 'What did . . . [A] mean to you that you felt so . . . [C] about it?' What you are trying to get is an inference and an evaluation of A. If the client doesn't give it to you, or gives you another A, you can ask more specifically: 'What was it about . . . [A] that upset you? Was it something bad?'

8 Write down the client's answer in the dysfunctional B column. Show the client as you write, and explain.

9 Repeat actions (7) and (8) until you have several thoughts, including at least one evaluation.

10 Ask the client if his thoughts about A would make him feel the way he did at C. Here the counsellor is beginning to point to the role of beliefs in producing emotional distress.
11 Recycle the procedure from (1) on another difficulty.

Case Example

1 *Counsellor*: Let's now focus on one of those difficulties you talked about and see if we can assess it in more detail. Which situation would you like to talk about?
Client: I'd like to talk about the restaurant again.
2 *Counsellor*: OK, let's take that situation. To start off with, can you tell me how you felt when you were last in the restaurant?
Client: Quite tense.
Counsellor: Quite tense?
Client: Well very tense. I felt sick, and just wanted to get out.
3 *Counsellor*: Mhm. So you felt very tense, you felt sick and you wanted to escape from the place. I'll write down here in the C column . . . [*Introduces and explains the ABC form.*] Is that description accurate? [*Client nods.*]
4 *Counsellor*: Tell me a few details about what happened?
Client: Well, people were looking at me. They're always staring at me.
5 *Counsellor*: I'll write down here in the A column 'People looked and stared at me', if that's accurate.
6 *Counsellor*: In summary then, you say you felt very tense and sick because people were looking and staring at you. [*Client confirms.*]
7 *Counsellor*: What thoughts did you have at the time – when people were looking at you and you felt that way?
Client: They're looking at me in a funny way.
8 *Counsellor*: I'll write that down here in the 'dysfunctional' B column. [*Explains 'dysfunctional'.*] As you see the B comes between the A and the C.
9 *Counsellor*: What other thoughts did you have?
Client: They think I'm weird.
10 *Counsellor*: Do you think it was that idea, that belief 'They think I'm weird' that was making you very tense about going to the restaurant again?
Client: Certainly it did.
Counsellor: But you wouldn't be tense if you'd said: 'It doesn't bother me what they think of me.' What were you saying to yourself?
Client [*beginning to look tearful*]: I believe they're right – I *am* weird.
[*Counsellor continues recording and explores how the last belief is the one that causes real distress.*]

The counsellor then explores two more emotional episodes and writes them out on ABC forms – one in which the client got extremely anxious at work because he knew he had made a mistake in a report, and another in which he was shaking while playing snooker. In both assessments, the main inferences were that people were critical of him, leading him to extremely negative self-evaluation.

Reaching an Initial Formulation

We have so far made use of the ABC model as an aid to obtaining the main components of information from the client – the activating events, the beliefs, and the emotional and behavioural consequences. But, of course, as we have seen, the model is much more powerful than this. It gives us a cognitive theory to explain the reason for the client's problems. So the next task is to use the model to make tentative hypotheses, some of which may form the basis of CB intervention.

The structure of the hypothesis will already be familiar: the client will be making inferences and evaluations about the As through a set of Bs which lead to emotional and behavioural Cs. This simple model forms the basis of all the counsellor's hypotheses. The key component in these hypotheses is the B – which in CBC is the primary reason for the distress and the maladaptive behaviour.

Of course, each ABC episode has its own specific B, and we could simply focus our assessment on each of these specific Bs, but it is more valuable to look for more generalised themes underlying the beliefs. One of the reasons we have recommended getting several ABC assessments before beginning the process of intervention is that this will help the counsellor to arrive at the client's generalised (rather than specific) inferential and evaluative style of thinking. For example, a client might have a series of beliefs: 'If Mrs Jones ignores me that will prove I'm not likeable'; 'If I make a mistake that will show I'm useless'; 'John knows I'm no good – he gave me a funny look'. However there may be a single belief underlying all three, to the effect that 'I must have everyone's approval in order to be a worthwhile person.' It is this generalised, core belief that we try to identify in a formulation. A formulation tentatively asserts that the client has one or more general, dysfunctional beliefs underlying several specific emotional episodes.

As the assessment progresses, the counsellor, in her own mind, will want to sharpen up a few of her hypotheses into such formulations. The counsellor will start to think about possible formulations as she changes her interviewing style from wide-ranging exploration to more specific questioning based around the ABC model, and the use of the ABC form. The answers to the specific questions will contribute to the evidence that will support or refute her formulations, leading to better ones. It will be noticed that the development of formulations reflects exactly CBC theory – the empirical and logical testing of ideas or beliefs and modifying or discarding them accordingly.

The counsellor's task now is to try to select one or more provisional 'working' formulations, based on the client's ABC assessments and which she senses may be psychologically acceptable to the client initially as a basis for starting the work of change in counselling. These formulations should also be specific enough to form the basis of goals and tasks to be developed later. As counselling progresses the counsellor will usually find that the formulations change, often several times, as more information leads to more fundamental beliefs. This points up the need to be tentative and flexible.

Action Summary
1 During the exploration phase, the counsellor goes over in her mind, or jots down, various tentative hypotheses about beliefs that might explain the client's difficulties.
2 She firms up in her mind, on the basis of evidence, one or more of the more significant hypotheses to direct her ABC assessments.
3 She uses CB theory to structure her formulation, namely in terms of the client's ABCs. In this structure, (C) is the problem (dysfunctional emotion or behaviour or both), (B) is the primary reason for the problem, and (A) is the activating event. She bases her formulation on a sample of several ABC assessments.

Case Example
3 In the first ABC assessment, Andrew is anxious (C) about going into a cafe (A) and thinks people will realise that he is weird (B). A tentative, general formulation is that Andrew's anxiety is determined by his tendency to misinterpret the reactions of others and evaluate himself negatively in social situations. Couched in these general terms, the formulation also explains the other two assessments – his worry about his report, and his shakiness while playing snooker. The counsellor always ensures her formulation is based on the client's stated problems. She also assesses whether the client will be able to accept it as the basis of a working formulation, that is, as the basis for cognitive intervention.

Helping the Client Understand
The counsellor has so far carried out part of her cognitive assessment, and made a tentative formulation, but she does not keep this to herself. The client too usually has his own theory about his problem, and if this is different from the counsellor's, not much progress will be made. The idea is to offer CBC as an alternative theory, so he can make an informed decision about whether it helps to explain his problem, and hence that CBC makes sense as an approach to finding a solution.

A further purpose of helping the client understand his problem in CBC terms is that this understanding will maximise the client's potential to help himself in the future and become less dependent on the counsellor. This places CBC squarely in the self-help school. If successful, it helps improve the client's sense of self-effectiveness, by enabling the client to attribute the cause of change to his own efforts. This is extremely important since clients often feel helpless and worthless when they seek counselling, and this demoralisation is a significant, if not major, part of the problem (Frank, 1961). There is a danger that a counsellor, acting as the expert who will 'cure' the patient, may exacerbate the problem, in that the client will then attribute the cause of any beneficial change to the counsellor and any failure to change to himself, and remain demoralised. CBC, then, is essentially a collaborative enterprise, seeking to mobilise the client's own resources and restore his sense of self-effectiveness.

The counsellor's task, after doing an ABC assessment, is to share her formulation in an explanatory summary of the client's As, Bs and Cs. The summary should teach the client that it is the B that 'causes' his C, not the A, at least not the A alone. To achieve this goal, the counsellor will find it useful to use one of the client's ABC assessments that she previously wrote down on the ABC form, and explain the meaning of the A, B and C. In this way she can use the client's own situations and emotional responses, and reveal the mediating role of the client's beliefs between the two. Hints on how this can be done will be found in the action summary and case example below.

If the client has difficulty understanding the role of beliefs using the above approach, there are a number of techniques for showing the client the role of thoughts. One is to give the client a situation and ask him what he would have to be thinking to be anxious or depressed or angry about it. For example:

A: It is 10 p.m. and there is a knock at the door.
C: You feel anxious.
B: You're thinking: — — — — — — —
or
C: You feel angry.
B: You're thinking: — — — — — — —

Another is to get the client to imagine first an unpleasant and then a pleasant situation and report his thoughts after each. Whatever way is chosen, the counsellor will always return to the client's own problem, to ensure he understands how the model fits his own case.

Action Summary

1 Ask the client to select one of the ABC assessments. With the relevant form in front of you, suggest to the client that you should

now go over the selected episode again together, and while doing so, try to identify, and agree, the 'cause' of the difficulty. Assuming the client agrees, then:

2 Ask the client to confirm the A and C.
3 Ask the client to confirm B.
4 Ask the client to confirm what caused C. 'Was it A or B?'
5 Whichever answer is given, ask the client 'How?'
6 If A is given, continue to ask 'How?' until a definite belief (inference and/or evaluation rather than fact) is given, and show that this is really a B. Then repeat step (4).
7 Check out that it makes sense to the client that it is the B that generates C rather than A.
8 Recycle the procedure for two or more assessments.
9 Discuss any common beliefs for all examples, and offer your own formulation.

Case Example

1 *Counsellor*: Let's summarise together this ABC assessment of the restaurant situation. And let's try to identify, and agree, the cause of your problem in that situation.
2 *Counsellor*: We've got under C that you felt sick and very tense, and under A that people kept looking at you in that situation.
   Client: That's right.
3 *Counsellor*: We've also got under B that you thought people were looking at you in a funny way, and that you believed that people thought you were weird.
   Client: That's right.
4 *Counsellor*: Right. Let me ask you then, what do you think is responsible for C – those feelings? Was it A or B?
   Client: Well, as I said it was being in the restaurant, and having people look at me.
5 *Counsellor*: How would that (points to the statement, under A) get you so worried?
   Client: Well, because as I said, they think I'm weird.
6 *Counsellor*: And how would that (points to B) make you so sick with worry?
   Client: Well, because if that's what they think it must be true.
7 *Counsellor*: So if you're convinced by the thought 'they think I'm weird and they're right' (points to B), that is quite enough to upset you like that (points to C). Does it make sense that that belief in itself can upset you?
   Client: It certainly does.
8 [*Client and counsellor then review the work example and the snooker example.*]
9 [*The counsellor then asks the client for a common theme in the three examples, and finally shares with him her own formulation.*]

Initial Cognitive Intervention

How does the counsellor make the transition from assessment to intervention? How does she decide what problems to work on? What techniques should she use? Assessment and intervention are part of the same process, and progression from one to the other should be logical and natural. This is the case in CBC, where a good assessment should inform client and counsellor what to focus on and in what way. The client has selected priority problem areas, and ABC assessments and formulations have been made. In this section we shall show how to use this information to help the client start to work at real change.

There are four steps in this process, the first two in this section, the third and fourth in the closing phase. The steps are: (1) agreeing the method of working; (2) the selection of goals to work on; (3) the selection of tasks to achieve the goals; and (4) agreeing the 'boundary conditions'.

First, the counsellor has to find out if the ABC way of formulating problems has face validity for the client. Does he find it persuasive? Is it a good basis for working on his difficulties? If so, then counsellor and client need to agree on specific working formulations, preferably, but not necessarily, those previously worked out.

Secondly, using the working formulations as a guide, the client selects initial, specific goals he wishes to work on.

Thirdly, client and counsellor agree on some initial tasks designed to achieve the goals, and these then become the first homework assignments, for example, data gathering by diary-keeping, monitoring and recording behaviour, thought and emotion.

Fourthly, client and counsellor agree the boundary conditions. Client and counsellor negotiate the number, frequency and length of sessions, agenda for sessions, role relationship, and locus of responsibility.

Negotiating the ABC Way of Formulating Problems
Progress from assessment to intervention is dependent on there being an agreed understanding between counsellor and client on the client's problems. The approach offered should also appeal to the client, and have good face validity. To achieve these aims, in CBC we seek to get the client's endorsement of, as well as understanding of, the ABC approach to formulating those problems. This then provides the framework and rationale, and improves the motivation, for the hard and often uncomfortable work that is to follow. It also helps, as we have seen, to ensure that the work of counselling is collaborative, that counsellor and client are following the same 'blueprint' or treatment plan and agree on the steps that have to be followed. The

counsellor may not, of course, need to negotiate a common approach with the client, who may already have signalled his endorsement, even enthusiasm, during the ABC assessment. However, experience tells us that the counsellor should check out this common agreement, for the client may well have his own theory about his problems, and have covertly rejected the counsellor's approach.

Action Summary
1 Summarise the ABC method and philosophy so far followed in the assessment, and ask for the client's reaction to this.
2 If necessary explore the client's objections, and his own approach if different. Spell out the advantages of the CBC approach.
3 If the client agrees, ask how he thinks it might be helpful.
4 If the client agrees but is sceptical, acknowledge the doubts but suggest a trial run. If necessary describe (anonymously) how other clients utilised CBC successfully (though be sure to warn the client there are no guarantees of success).
5 Take one of the ABC assessments previously worked out and ensure it is an agreed working formulation of a problem situation.

Case Example
1 *Counsellor*: What we've been doing is looking at your difficulties using the ABC method. In other words we've broken those difficulties down into A, events that happened (or might happen) to you; B, your inference and evaluation of the events; and C, how you consequently felt and reacted. We've also said that B, your beliefs, may very well have a big role to play in C – how you felt and reacted. Before we go any further, tell me what you honestly think of this way of looking at your difficulties?
Client: Yes I think it's helpful.
3 *Counsellor*: That's good. In what way is it helpful?
Client: Well I might be looking at things negatively. I might be able to look at things more positively. But I'm not sure I can.
4 *Counsellor*: So you think it might be helpful to learn to look at things in a better way, but you have your doubts.
Client: That's right. But I'll give it a go.
4 *Counsellor*: Shall we then have a go at using the ABC method for the next step – which is to look at ways of overcoming your difficulties?
Client: Sure, I'd like to try that.
5 *Counsellor*: Good. well let's take the restaurant situation again, and see if we agree on the ABC method of formulating that problem.

Negotiating Goals
By this stage the counsellor and client should be sharing a common understanding and agreed method of working. Everything is at last ready for initiating therapeutic change. The counsellor starts by establishing that the client's goal is to change his emotional and

behavioural reaction, and ensuring that the client understands that cognitive change is the most potent means of producing emotional and behavioural change. Then, rather than challenging and disputing the client's expressed beliefs at this stage – this procedure will form a major part of stage 2 in the next chapter – the counsellor simply asks the client to think of more helpful alternatives to his habitual thoughts, and to judge how the alternatives would make him feel and react. Clients often show themselves to be quite resourceful in suggesting realistic alternatives, and this method helps develop the client's capacity to change. However, the counsellor can also suggest alternatives, and get the client to assess their credibility. The counsellor will find many more ways of developing alternative thinking in stage 2.

Clients will often say that they have less faith in the alternative thoughts than their usual negative ones. However, it is usually the case that clients will have *some* faith in the alternatives, and in practice will get benefit from rehearsing and using these in real situations – the topic of the next section. More powerful ways of discrediting negative thinking and bolstering realistic thinking will be given in stage 2.

We often find that clients may still focus on changing A as the best way of changing C. One way of dealing with this is to acknowledge that changing A is indeed a way of changing C – if Andrew can somehow stop people looking at him (if they are) or if he avoids times when there are lots of people around (as he does) then he will feel better at C. But, the counsellor can emphasise, you cannot always influence the behaviour of others, or always choose the best times (when, for example, the restaurant is empty), but you can alter your inferences and evaluations of the behaviour of others, and this approach gives you a method of coping which is quite independent of what other people do.

Action Summary
1 Stay with one of the specific ABC assessments, and clarify that the client's emotional and behavioural problem comes under C, and that his goal is to change C.
2 Ask the client how, on the basis of the discussion, he could change the problem – by changing A or B?
3 If necessary help the client see that changing B is the more powerful way of changing C.
4 Ask the client if he can think of any more helpful alternatives to the first thought listed under B on the ABC form for the situation under discussion. Write these down in the second column under B (functional alternative thought). If necessary suggest some

alternatives and write these down if the client agrees they are reasonable.

5 Ask the client if the emotional and behavioural problem under C *still* follows from the alternative thought(s) just listed. If not, ask the client what consequence *would* follow from the alternative thought, and write this down in the second C column (functional consequence). However, if the client says that the same problematic consequence follows, repeat step 4.

6 If the client says that he has no faith in the alternative thought and it does not help him, then ask him to weigh the evidence for the two thoughts – the original dysfunctional thought and the functional alternative(s). This step anticipates stage 2 and is dealt with thoroughly in that section (Chapter 3) and also in Chapter 5.

Case Example

1 *Counsellor*: We've done some ABC assessments, and we've agreed a way of working. Now let's get started on changing some of those problems. I suggest we stay with the restaurant situation and then tackle some others. [*Client nods.*] Let me clarify first what I think we are doing and you correct me if I am wrong. The problem is how you feel (very tense) and how you behave (avoidantly) in the restaurant situation. If you remember we put those bad feelings and unhelpful behaviours under C (dysfunctional consequence) on the form here. [*Client nods.*] Now your *goal* is to change those feelings and ways of behaving for better ones. [*Client assents.*]

2 *Counsellor*: Let me ask you how you might best go about changing those feelings and ways of behaving – would it be by changing the activating event itself, A or would it be by changing the beliefs?

Client: Changing my beliefs would be effective, but I don't see that there is any other way of thinking about it.

4 *Counsellor*: That is understandable, but I think there is. Let's take the first B you have here [*points to first dysfunctional thought under B*]: 'They looked at me in a funny way.' Can you think of a more helpful alternative? What comes to mind?

Client: [*pause*] what about, 'I was imagining they were looking at me in a funny way but I also regard myself as a rather insignificant person and they probably didn't even notice me.'

Counsellor: [*Ignoring for the moment the client's view of himself as an insignificant person and focuses on his alternative thought that they probably didn't notice him.*] Does that seem a reasonable alternative? Could it be true that they probably didn't notice you?

Client: Yes, it could be true.

Counsellor: OK, then I'll write that down here in the functional alternative column.

5 *Counsellor*: So, we have the alternative thought 'I was imagining they were looking at me in a funny way but actually they might not have even noticed me.' In the C column though we have the old dysfunctional

consequence of 'very tense' and 'want to get out'. Does that follow from the new thought?

Client: No. What would follow would be much milder than that, I would still feel a bit tense but I probably wouldn't want to leave.

Counsellor: In that case I'll write that down here in the functional C column.

Counsellor and client continue to obtain some further alternative thoughts, which are also listed, together with their alternative consequences.

CLOSING PHASE

The closing phase has two sections – one to set up the homework the client should preferably do as a result of completing stage 1, and the other to establish the conditions for future counselling interviews and stages, often known as the 'boundary' conditions.

Negotiating Homework Tasks

We have reached the stage of helping the client to change his Bs by the method of alternative thoughts. The next step is to help the client start to put this into practice between the end of this interview and the beginning of the next. One procedure for doing this is to get the client to rehearse thoroughly the alternative thoughts for a problematic situation, and then try 'talking to himself' in the actual situation, using the alternatives. This simple method can work quite straightforwardly, and is definitely worth trying without unnecessarily complicating the procedure. We outline the steps in the action summary.

However, the counsellor should anticipate that in future interviews there are likely to be one or more of a variety of problems which commonly occur and require modifications to the basic procedure. We will mention two in particular. The first is that the client may be so absorbed by his habitual way of thinking, he cannot draw on, or even remember the alternatives. This problem is dealt with in stage 2. The second is that the client may fail to go into some of the more difficult situations where he can rehearse his new thinking, because of anticipatory anxiety. This problem is dealt with in detail in stage 3. At this introductory stage it is best simply to get the client to attempt 'real life' *in vivo* homework assignments, to warn him that he may not initially be successful, and to tell him that unsuccessful attempts are important steps on the way to successful attempts. Unsuccessful attempts at carrying out difficult homework assignments, and even serious intentions that get no further than preparation, throw up new sets of dysfunctional beliefs which can also be dealt with in CBC, and which will in their turn be the focus of intervention (they will be discussed in stage 3). At this stage the counsellor can reassure the client that CBC necessarily proceeds in stages, from initially getting started, through learning new insights, and finally overcoming blocks to change and independence. The client can be forewarned that he will probably experience these stages, and to allow time for this to happen.

Action Summary
1 The counsellor asks the client to agree to go into one or more of the difficult situations (the A of the ABC) for which he now has some alternative thoughts.
2 The counsellor shows the client how to prepare himself for introducing the new thinking into the problem situation. This involves practice in imagination, and the client is advised to set aside a quiet half-an-hour each day to do it. He is to rehearse the new thoughts so that he can recall them effortlessly. Next he imagines being in the problem situation, and runs through the new thoughts. He practises this procedure until it is fairly automatic.
3 The client undertakes to enter the situation at a specified time, and repeat what he has rehearsed for real.
4 After carrying out the assignment, the client agrees to note down (a) how successful/unsuccessful he was in producing the new thinking in the actual situation; (b) whether he was successful or not in changing his dysfunctional feelings and behaviour in the actual situation.
5 The client repeats steps 1 to 4 for the same situation at least three times, even if he is unsuccessful. The client may also carry out the same routine for other problem situations, though the counsellor will want to guard against overloading the client.

Case Example
1 *Counsellor*: You have been very resourceful in providing alternative thoughts to the ones you usually have. But they won't help you too much if you can't use them in the situations that trouble you. So first, you have to try to go and put yourself back in those situations, and second take the new thoughts with you. Do you see any problems in doing those things?
   Client: I'm going to find it very difficult to do either of those things.
   Counsellor: How about going back into one of those situations – can you face the restaurant for example?
   Client: I suppose I can try.
   Counsellor: All I urge is that you seriously try. You should be able to manage some of these situations, and if you can learn the alternative thoughts, they should help.
2 *Counsellor*: Coming to the second point, there is a way you can learn the

alternative thoughts well, and so get ready for using them in the real situation. If you like, I'll suggest a procedure which we can try out together now for a situation you choose. After that you may like to try it out at home, and practise it for, say, about half-an-hour a day . . .

3 *Counsellor*: You agreed you would try to go into the difficult situation you chose. Let's now agree, then, on the day and time you will enter it . . .

4 *Counsellor*: My last request is that you make a note of how you get on in the situation . . . [*See step 4 above.*]

There are a number of alternative types of homework. Chapter 6 is a resource chapter for homework techniques, and the counsellor will find it useful to familiarise herself with these, so that she may respond flexibly and appropriately at this crucial point in the first stage of CBC.

Negotiating the Boundary Conditions

Counsellor and client have nearly reached the end of stage 1 – getting started. Before concluding this stage – and this interview, counsellor and client need to stand back from the detailed work of counselling and to come to some agreement on the boundaries and ground rules of their relationship. The whole of the therapeutic enterprise needs to have 'boundaries' or ground rules. One reason for boundaries is practical – every referral entails a certain amount of administration, and there are limited resources which have to be efficiently deployed. But another reason is to safeguard the development of a therapeutic relationship and not some other kind of relationship. The client may bring unrealistic beliefs, expectations and needs to counselling, mis-interpret the counsellor's behaviour and attempt to draw the counsellor into the kind of dysfunctional relationship that may have contributed to the client's problem in the first place. The boundary conditions ensure a framework of objectivity, throw into sharper relief the client's 'projections' or belief system, and ensure the counsellor stays on the periphery of the client's actual life. For these and other reasons, client and counsellor must negotiate the number, frequency and length of sessions, agenda for sessions, the principle of collaboration, the principle of a contract and, if necessary, the role relationships between them. Most of these tasks are fortunately fairly simple and straightforward, but can go wrong and guidelines are often helpful. Here, the counsellor is recommended to read an intro-ductory book on this topic, such as Storr (1979). The following are minimal recommendations for setting up boundary conditions.

1 *Number of sessions*. We suggest six to ten initially, with a review at the end of the period. This communicates that counselling is not totally open-ended, but is open-ended enough to ensure reaching some sort of therapeutic 'closure'.

2 *Frequency of sessions*. We suggest once a week, or more frequently in the case of crises. Less frequent contact strains continuity and decreases the likelihood of keeping the client to the 'contract'.

3 *Length of sessions*. We suggest the traditional fifty minute hour – long enough to get 'depth' in interviewing but not long enough to get too tired! Keeping strictly to the allotted number, frequency and length of sessions is important to help ensure that the counsellor is not drawn into ever-longer commitments, unhelpful 'games' or nonlegitimate relationships.

4 *Agenda setting*. This is a good time to *introduce* the idea of an agenda for future sessions, so as to prepare the client to expect this at the next interview. The details of agenda setting will be dealt with later in the book. At this point it is necessary only to explain the rationale to the client – that an agenda ensures that major issues are not neglected and that the sessions stay relevant to the client's needs. It is useful to suggest that both counsellor and client give some thought to the agenda for the next session.

5 *Principle of collaboration*. This is also a good time to negotiate the principle of collaboration, again so as to prepare the client to expect this mode of practice in future counselling sessions. It can be presented as a 'team' effort in which the client undertakes to collect the 'raw data' (Beck et al., 1979) and work hard at change and in which the counsellor undertakes to guide the client and provide him with psychological support.

6 *Principle of a contract*. The principle of collaboration is underpinned by a formal or informal contract. Behavioural counsellors often prefer a formal contract, which can be a written document specifying the undertakings of both parties, with some penalty for failure to comply and a reward for complying with the contract. The purpose of a written contract is to encourage the client to carry out often extremely difficult homework assignments. An alternative is an informal contract, but with explicit agreements about the principle of collaboration, and with the specific detailing of tasks to be undertaken. This is often sufficient to gain compliance, is more flexible and imposes less strain on the therapeutic alliance.

We have now reached the end of stage 1. The counsellor will now want to take the client on to the next stage, the main aim of which is to help the client gain deeper insight and more robust behavioural and emotional change, as well as to learn the method of CBC itself.

3 Stage 2: Teaching the Cognitive-Behavioural Method of Change

The second stage of CBC has two main tasks for the counsellor. The first is to help the client to consolidate and make further progress in overcoming his emotional and behavioural problems through CBC. The second is to help the client to learn the theory and method of CBC itself, so that he may gain insight into his difficulties, and increasingly take the initiative in assessing and resolving them. In order to address these tasks, this, the main stage of CBC, contains the following phases.

Opening Phase

Preliminary Enquiries
This starts stage two when the counsellor invites the client to bring up pressing issues, when counsellor and client agree on a session agenda, and when the client is invited to give feedback on the counselling so far, and homework carried out.

Middle Phase

Cognitive Assessment
This is when the counsellor carries out a comprehensive and in-depth cognitive assessment, including teaching the client the assessment method.

Cognitive Intervention
This is when the counsellor carries out comprehensive disputation of the client's unhelpful beliefs, and teaches the client the method of disputing.

Closing Phase

Negotiating Homework Tasks
This is when counsellor and client renegotiate the important tasks for working on at home or work, including the incorporation of alternative thinking.

We suggest that the counsellor structures her interviews according to the three phases, but plans to devote several interviews to the material contained in stage 3, much as we recommend in stage 2. In this chapter we again provide case examples based on our client Andrew. We again emphasise that the examples are mainly provided for the purpose of illustrating one particular way of counselling, and not a hard and fast rule as to how the counsellor should proceed.

At this point in CBC, the client should have been through a complete cycle of induction and exploration, assessment and intervention, and finally to have attempted some homework tasks. What now? Should the counsellor start a completely new set of procedures? Should she be dealing with deeper and more mysterious and difficult problems? Should she be giving profound insights and advice? In fact she does none of these things. What she has to do is much simpler and obvious – she repeats the cycle of the first stage, with an exploratory opening, an assessment and intervention middle period, and a homework-setting closing phase. The first stage has built the foundations, and the subsequent stages build upon that, and this means following the same structure.

In that case, what are the differences between the first and second stages? The main difference is that the second stage introduces more powerful techniques for assessment and intervention, including ways of identifying elusive beliefs and distinguishing types of beliefs, and methods of challenging and disputing dysfunctional beliefs.

The counsellor should be able to spend less time establishing a therapeutic relationship with the client. As the routine becomes familiar, the client should feel more secure, and know what to expect and what to do. There is some less risk of losing the client, and the building of rapport with the client can begin to take less of the centre ground. The counsellor can spend less time in exploration and more in in-depth cognitive assessment and intervention. More time is spent in eliciting and challenging unhelpful client beliefs, planning of 'experiments', and engaging the client in tasks designed to improve insight, motivation and behaviour change. However, the therapeutic alliance must be continuously monitored, and the counsellor needs to pay particular attention to her continued unconditional acceptance of the client, and to continue to probe the client's attitude to counselling and the counsellor.

OPENING PHASE

Preliminary Enquiries

At the beginning of the second stage the counsellor establishes continuity, maintains contact with the client's thoughts and feelings about counselling, and prepares the ground for this stage. Specifically the counsellor (1) asks if there are any pressing problems the client wants to talk about initially; (2) establishes a session agenda; (3) invites feedback on the previous stage and interviews; and (4) requests an update on the problems and the homework. These steps should be used flexibly, and are suggested only as a possible way of structuring the beginning of stage 2.

Pressing Problems
It is always best to offer the client the initiative to open each interview. This is simply an extension of good counselling skills, and ensures that the client has the opportunity to talk about pressing issues. If the client does have a pressing concern, the counsellor is advised to give the client the time he needs to discuss this before going on to the next steps, even if this means postponing these steps to the next interview. The client may well be so preoccupied with a problem that he will not focus on the counsellor's agenda until the issue is addressed. However, the counsellor should be aware that some clients may flit from one pressing problem to the next – not leaving time for investigation into core long-term problems.

Session Agenda
An agenda is a useful structure for ensuring that major topics and tasks are not overlooked and the time is allocated in a planned way (a common problem is that without an agenda time runs out before homework tasks are set). It can be used as a 'facilitator' with restrained clients and a 'constrainer' with verbose clients. It also establishes a 'ground rule' and hence gives the counsellor open-ended 'permission' to interrupt and otherwise guide the client. The agenda can include as topic headings any or all of the tasks we have identified here in the second stage: pressing problems, feedback on counselling so far, homework report, plus the selection of one or two main problems for this session, and setting the next homework. The counsellor is advised not to be overambitious in what she tries to include.

Feedback
The client may now be more prepared to talk about his experience of the first stage interviews. He will also have had time to evaluate the purpose of the first stage. The client's attitude, and willingness to be engaged in the second stage, is very dependent on his perception of the first. This is also an opportunity to explain to the client what the second stage of counselling will consist of.

Report on Homework
Routinely requesting a report on homework ensures continuity, and

starts to establish a pattern which will mark all future interviews. It gets the client into a 'monitoring' habit which is essential for cognitive and behaviour change. A homework report should, of course, usually form an integral part of the update. It is poor counselling practice to forget to ask for a report on homework – the client will think that his painful efforts are not valued, and his motivation will be affected. It is also most important to investigate non-defensively failures to carry out homework – the reasons will form the substance of part of the present counselling session. The client should be reassured that attempting but failing to carry out homework assignments is as important and useful as attempting and succeeding. Unsuccessful attempts highlight problematic beliefs that might otherwise be much more difficult to elucidate. It is often wise to put aside considerable counselling time in the second stage for dealing with negative client beliefs about failure in homework. We recommend that at this point the counsellor reads Chapter 6 on 'Homework Tasks' which provides a framework and a number of suggestions on setting homework.

Action Summary
1 Greet the client and invite him to begin by talking about any pressing problems.
2 If the client seems ready, suggest that you establish an agenda, giving reasons for this. Make a list of agenda items. Include feedback, a report on homework, choosing one or more problems for assessment and cognitive intervention, and preparing homework for the next interview.
3 Ask the client for his assessment of the first stage interviews, and his assessment of the direction of counselling. Say that you would like to move on to the second stage and explain briefly what this is.
4 Ask the client to bring you up to date on the problems talked about during the first stage, and to give you a report on his homework.
5 Ask the client to select one or two main problems for this session.

Case Example
1 *Counsellor* [*after greeting the client*]: Is there anything on your mind right now that you'd like to talk about first today?
  Client: Nothing particularly pressing I suppose, though there are a number of things really – it's difficult to know where to start.
2 *Counsellor*: One way we could proceed today, and in the next sessions, is to write down the things we both think should be covered, so that nothing important is forgotten. How do you feel about a kind of agenda like that?
  Client: Yes, OK.
  Counsellor: Let's try it.
  [*An agreed general framework includes pressing problems, feedback, homework report, one or two main problems, and new homework.*]

3 *Counsellor*: You've completed the first stage of CBC now, culminating last week in some homework tasks. What's your opinion of it so far?

   Client: Well it all makes some better sense than it did. I feel more optimistic, but not a lot, yet. I can see that the way I think about events makes them worse ... [*Elaborates*.]

   Counsellor: I'm glad you feel counselling is helping and that you're a bit more optimistic. You accept that your thinking is important in contributing to how you feel, and that's an important point. [*Describes the purpose of the second stage and explains how it builds on the first*.]

4 *Counsellor*: Let's now review how things are going. Tell me how your difficulties have been since we last met, and about the homework we agreed to.

   Client: Well I did go back to the restaurant but had all the old problems as you see on this form. I just couldn't help thinking they were all looking at me. I couldn't remember the alternative thought.

   Counsellor: Were you looking around to check if they were looking at you?

   Client: No I was avoiding looking at them.

   Counsellor: [*Elicits and suggests ideas for new homework*.] Let me summarise what we have agreed you could try. Write the alternative thought on the back of a visiting card and keep it in the palm of your hand or handy in your top pocket. Every time you feel tense and get the automatic thought, look at the card. Secondly check it out – casually look around you and see what people are doing. Thirdly, try this in a lot more places, such as just walking down the street.

5 *Counsellor*: Let's now put on the agenda one or two main problems you'd like to deal with today. What would you like to select?

   Client: Well, there is a particular problem I'd like to talk about today. It's to do with joining an evening class. I feel so terrible I think I'll have to stop going. I'd like some help on that.

MIDDLE PHASE

Cognitive Assessment

In stage 1 we described how to use the ABC method to analyse the client's problems. We showed how to extract significant emotional episodes from the general picture of these problems, to identify the A, B and C components (though preferably in the order C, A and B), and how, by changing the B, we could change the C.

However, to make further progress in stage 2, it is now necessary to review the ABC assessment model in general, and clarify its components in particular.

The ABC model is about the *process* of human adaptation (and maladaptation) to the environment. People appraise events around them, and then respond to those events as they see them. They respond both emotionally (because those events may seem life-enhancing or life-threatening) and behaviourally (because of what people believe they could and should do about them).

The appraisal of events involves not only a hunch about what is actually happening or is likely to happen – an inference – but also a judgment about how good or bad that event is for the individual concerned – an evaluation. This appraisal has a significance for the client in terms of whether the event is likely to help or endanger him, causing him to react emotionally and to attempt, if necessary, to cope with the event. Such coping responses will vary more or less in how successful they are, and how successfully the individual perceives they are. A person's distress will depend not only on the degree of threat that he sees in an event, but his confidence in how well he believes he can cope with that threat.

It will be clear from this outline of the ABC model that there are important differences within the A, B, and C components, particularly, for example, between different kinds of Bs, and between different kinds of emotional and behavioural Cs. We now need to address these differences, and clarify the distinction *between* the components, particularly between As and Bs on the one hand, and Cs and Bs on the other. Finally we need to deal with the problem of helping the client to get access to core dysfunctional cognitions that are extremely elusive and difficult to retrieve. In this section we shall show how to identify different kinds of As, Bs and Cs, how to discriminate between these components, and introduce one powerful method of eliciting inferences and evaluations. We shall proceed in the recommended order for carrying out the assessment, and we recommend that the counsellor use the ABC assessment form to help make and record her clarifications.

Clarifying Cs

The counsellor's main task in clarifying the Cs is to get a factually accurate account of the client's emotional and behavioural reactions to appraised events. Since the client will not usually be very clear about his Cs, the counsellor will often need to undertake some detailed questioning and facilitating. We give below some guidelines on how to identify types and intensities of C and how to distinguish them.

Emotional Cs
We pointed out in stage 1 that there were two types of Cs, emotional and behavioural. We will now describe each of these in more detail, beginning with emotional Cs.

We need to distinguish between *types* of emotional Cs and to assess the *intensity* of the emotional Cs, when carrying out ABC assessments.

Types of emotional Cs. People respond emotionally to significant events as they see them (the emotional C), feeling happy when things go well, and sad (for example) when things go badly. People generally seek counselling, however, when those feelings reach distressing proportions.

One of the counsellor's first tasks is to identify exactly what emotion the client is experiencing. Clients often do not or cannot express clearly the emotion they experience about an event. For example the client may report feeling upset, but does this mean he feels anxious or depressed, hurt, guilty or ashamed, or something else? As a rough and ready rule of thumb there are three primary negative emotions, namely anxiety, anger and depression, with numerous secondary emotions which are derived from these, such as guilty depression or shameful depression. For each emotion people also have a threshold or tolerance level at which point the emotion is triggered, so that the client with a very low threshold will react very quickly to minor levels of aversiveness – for example, the person who reacts angrily to the slightest inconvenience, or panics at the slightest twinge or pain. Rational-emotive theorists refer to this as low frustration tolerance (LFT). It is very important to identify correctly the type of emotion and the client's tolerance level towards that emotion, since these will help the counsellor target the relevant As and Bs.

Intensity of emotional Cs. Each of the primary emotions and their derivatives can vary in intensity from slight to severe, for example, from worried to terrified, sad to depressed, irritated to murderous rage. Usually it is only the intense emotions that are distressing and therefore a problem for the client. Thus it is very important for the counsellor to identify a strong, distressing emotion as the target emotion at C, since this will ensure she targets the relevant, faulty belief at B for her intervention. If the client describes his feelings in mild terms, the counsellor is advised to take great care in checking out that he really means he experiences this emotion only mildly, and if so, whether this is really a problem for him.

Bodily sensations and reactions. Bodily (physiological) sensations are usually an integral part of the experience of the emotional C and need to be carefully assessed. Both the type of emotion and its intensity can often be clarified by getting the client to describe these bodily sensations and reactions, particularly if the emotion is related to anxiety or anger.

Behavioural Cs

Types of behavioural Cs. People do not just respond emotionally to the events in their world (the emotional C); they also try, if necessary, to do something about them (the behavioural C). People seek help, not only when they feel emotionally distressed, but also when they feel their ways of coping are failing them.

After identifying the client's emotion, the counsellor's next task is to identify the client's faulty way of coping (the behavioural C). However, the behavioural C is usually functionally related to the emotion. Anxiety emotions are usually accompanied by avoidance or defensive behaviour, ranging from an extreme of avoiding or leaving situations, to less overt forms such as gaze aversion and other subtle non-verbal responses. Depression is accompanied by inactivity and withdrawal, and anger by overt or muted aggressive behaviour. These behavioural ways of coping with an event are nearly always dysfunctional, for though they may achieve a short-term effect, such as reducing stress by avoidance, in the longer term they maintain or worsen the problem.

Strength of behavioural Cs. The behavioural C will tend to be more exaggerated, overt and longer lasting if the emotional C is more intense. Such behaviour is liable to break social norms, and invite interpersonal censure of some kind. If the client's annoyance develops into anger, his behaviour may also overspill from assertion into aggression. If the client's sadness turns into depression, his expression of sadness may also turn into depressed behaviour, and research shows that depressed behaviour can be interpersonally aversive.

Distinguishing between the Cs

It is rare that the client gives the counsellor neatly distinguished emotional and behavioural Cs; he usually gives some more general description which combines the two. The counsellor's task is to distinguish between them. For example, if the client describes his C as 'I went to pieces', the client is helped to give a factual description in terms of emotional ('I felt panicky'), physiological ('I felt sick') and behavioural events ('I avoided looking at anybody'), not forgetting to reclassify 'went to pieces' as a cognitive label about those events – a point we come to in a moment.

Distinguishing Cs from Bs

Clients often describe their reaction to an A event in a single word or phrase, combining a B and C in the phrase. There are many words in English which combine emotional/behavioural (our C) elements, and cognitive elements. For example, clients may say they *feel* 'inadequate', 'helpless', 'stupid', 'useless', 'guilty' or 'ashamed' or 'a failure', as a consequence of some activating event. All these terms need to be separated into B and C elements. When the client describes a C event, the counsellor must make a careful distinction between that part which is cognitive (B) and that part which is emotive and/or behavioural (C). In the example above, the client labelled his C as 'went to pieces' which is clearly a cognitive label which has a metaphorical meaning but is not factually true. The client is taught to make this important distinction.

Action Summary
1   The counsellor invites the client to select an emotional episode – a current concern, or one that arose during homework, for example, and commences an ABC assessment.
2   The counsellor may first focus on clarifying the type and intensity of the emotional C and the accompanying physiological sensations, and explaining the distinctions to the client.
3   The counsellor can then focus on clarifying the type and intensity of the behavioural C.
4   The counsellor can distinguish, if necessary, between the emotional and behavioural Cs, and between Cs and Bs.
5   The Cs, once clarified, are written down in the dysfunctional C column of the ABC form.

Case Example
1   *Counsellor*: OK, Andrew, you said you would like to start with the problem you are having at your evening class. So let us do an ABC assessment using the usual form here. Perhaps to start with then, you could tell me about how you felt in that situation.
    Client: Well I really wished I hadn't gone. It was a terrible experience.
    Counsellor: What do you mean by 'terrible experience'?
    Client: Well it was just really awful.
2   *Counsellor*: Can you tell me what you actually felt?
    Client: Well I thought, 'What's wrong with me? Something terrible must be happening to me.'
4   *Counsellor*: So that's what you were thinking – that's a B and we can return to that in a moment. First, however, we need to get some more about the C. Tell me a bit about the experience itself – describe it exactly to me.
    Client: Oh yes, well I felt very, very tensed up.
4   *Counsellor*: Did you feel that physically or mentally?
    Client: Both I would say.
    Counsellor: Tell me about the physical sensations first.
    Client: It's difficult . . . I had this empty feeling . . .
2   *Counsellor*: An empty feeling? That doesn't sound like tension, perhaps that was how you felt later.
    Client: Oh yes that's right, I felt very depressed afterwards . . .
2   *Counsellor*: That's the C for another ABC episode that came later. But to return to the tense feeling – did you feel your heart pounding? Were you sweating? . . .
    Client: Certainly sweating, but it was more my tummy turning over and feeling sick. Even worse, I felt I might lose control of myself and actually be sick, you know.

3 *Counsellor*: I can understand that. I'll write this down now on the assessment form in the dysfunctional C column that you felt very tense, were sweating and felt nauseous. Now let us turn to the behavioural C. Can you give me a description of what you were doing exactly?
   Client: I was sitting very still and rigid, looking down, not daring to look at anyone ... etc. ...

Clarifying As

The task in clarifying As is to get the client to give as objective and factual an account as he can of the events that triggered the Cs. This requires that the counsellor be clear about types of As, and is able to clearly distinguish them from Bs and Cs.

Relevance of A to Cs

The first thing the counsellor has to establish, as we have shown in stage 1, is the relevance of A to C, as the next step in building a picture of an emotional episode. Clients easily wander to other events that are associated in their minds or talk of events in general terms. The counsellor gently directs the client's attention to the event that provided the context for the particular C described earlier. Of course, when the client prefers to start with an A, then the opposite applies – the counsellor has to ensure the C is relevant to the A.

Types of As

There is virtually no limit to what can be an A event. An A event is anything that a person attends to, appraises in some way at point B, and consequently reacts to at point C. The most straightforward A events are actual situations in the here-and-now world of the client, or events which are remembered or imagined. However, As can equally be a person's own feelings and behaviour (Cs can be As), or a person's own thoughts and beliefs (Bs can be As).
   Situations as As. People single out and make judgments about the day-to-day events that happen to them. Clients tend to have a biased perception of such events, focusing more on the negative rather than positive or neutral aspects of events. They may report, for example, events ranging from, say, a mild criticism by a friend to a physical assault by some aggressor, or a situation such as a crowded supermarket or an exposed place. The counsellor is advised to obtain a detailed and *factual* description of all aspects of the event. It is useful to assess events in terms of such parameters as time, place, situation, persons involved and verbal and non-verbal behaviour.
   Bs and Cs functioning as As. People focus not only on events that happen to them in their environments, but they also focus on their own beliefs (Bs function as As) and on their own emotional and

behavioural *reactions* to events (Cs function as As), and make judgments about those too. In the latter case, the C from one ABC can become the A for a second ABC. This is a particularly important type of A event for clients. A common experience is when the client feels anxious (C) about some event (A) but then feels anxious (new C) about the anxiety itself (now functioning as a new A), and so experiences anxiety about anxiety. Such cycles are quite common in practice, and can be quite confusing. It is useful to remember that clients commonly react to an event, and then react to their reaction, for example, 'I got scared, then I got angry that I got scared'. Cs functioning as As can also be factually and objectively assessed. They include, first, the client's feelings, which need to be distinguished and rated in terms of intensity, temporal occurrence, frequency, duration and associated situations. Secondly, they include the related physiological events which can be equally well assessed. Thirdly, they include the behavioural characteristics.

Equally common is when a B functions as an A. Here the client treats his own inference or evaluation as a fact, such as when the client below offers the 'fact' that his mother-in-law is a bitch. The way to proceed here is to make a clear separation of real As and Bs masquerading as As. We offer some advice below on distinguishing As and Bs.

Predicted As. Clients commonly forecast that an A event may, or will happen. This may be an event similar to one that has happened in the past, such as feeling faint in the supermarket, or it may be an event that has never actually happened, such as assault or rape.

Distinguishing As from Bs

Clients will not usually give their counsellors neatly clarified A events, but will more likely give statements which combine A with B. For example, if the client expresses anger at C, he may well offer an A, such as the mother-in-law being a bitch when she comes to visit. When the client describes an A event or situation in this way, the counsellor needs to make a distinction between fact on the one hand, and opinion, belief or imagination on the other, in the client's description. Having made the distinction, she needs to communicate this to the client. The aim is to help the client discriminate between 'subjective' descriptions of A events such as 'The mother-in-law was a bitch' and factual (or 'behavioural') descriptions like 'The mother-in-law did X on Saturday in the kitchen, Y on Sunday in the lounge etc.' The part of the description called 'bitch' can then more correctly be shown to belong to B, that is, the term 'bitch' is an evaluation of the mother-in-law rather than a description of her behaviour. Similarly, if the client describes a self-attributed A like 'I failed' (where C becomes A), the counsellor trains the client to redescribe the event in terms of the behavioural facts – *his* behaviour X and Y, and reclassify 'failed' to a B, namely a judgment *about* X and Y. We have already described how, in practice, the counsellor asks the client to be as specific and factual as possible.

Action Summary

1 The counsellor asks for a concrete description of the actual or imagined A event as part of an ABC assessment.
2 The counsellor distinguishes between fact and opinion (belief) in the client's description and points this out to the client.
3 The counsellor coaches the client in behavioural descriptions, specifying time, place, situation, individuals concerned and their behaviour.
4 The counsellor writes down in the A column of the ABC form the client's behavioural description.

Case Example

1 *Counsellor*: You told me how tense and sick you felt in the evening class, which we wrote down here under C. Let's now move to the A. Can you give me a concrete description of the situation and what happened.
 Client: I was sitting right in the middle of the class, surrounded by people, terrified that I'd be shown up for what I am.
2 *Counsellor*: OK, but only part of that sounds like a factual description (which may or may not be accurate), namely that you sat in the middle of the class, surrounded by people. However, the rest of what you said isn't part of the event or situation. It is partly your C – feeling terrified – and partly your B, that you would be shown up for what you are. Let's put under A only the facts, then put the beliefs under B on the form.
3 and 4 *Counsellor*: I'll write your description down while you describe the situation. It might help you to start at the moment you began to feel worse, and then to describe exactly what was happening.
 Client: OK, well it was about 7.30. It was crowded with people. The teacher was outlining the syllabus. Occasionally people would put their hands up and he would invite them to comment . . . etc. . . . .

Clarifying Bs

At this point the counsellor may like to bear in mind a corruption of the ancient saying that it is not events themselves that upset people but the views they take of them. In other words, the main task in clarifying Bs is to identify the beliefs by which the client views events such that those events become distressing for him. However, this is not an easy task. As the counsellor helps the client explore the Bs, with the help of the techniques described in stage 1, she will soon obtain a mass of potentially confusing statements, especially if the client is already in a state of confusion. The counsellor will find it helpful, therefore, if she can systematically distinguish between different types of beliefs, identify their functions, and assess those that are dysfunctional.

Relevance of Bs
The client has many beliefs of many kinds, and the counsellor needs to ensure that the beliefs she is seeking to identify are relevant to the emotional episode currently being assessed. She can achieve this by matching her B probes with the specific A and C that have already been established. A number of ways of probing for relevant Bs are given in the following examples.

Types of Bs
Without being aware of it, the client has two separate but connected types of thoughts about A events, namely inferences and evaluations. This is probably the most important of all the distinctions the counsellor will have to make. We will first describe the two types of Bs briefly, and then give a more detailed account of each.

Inferences. The first type of belief the client is likely to express is an interpretation of the event. We call this an inference, because it is a belief about what really happened or may happen, and may be true or false. For example, if someone walks to the other side of the road, one inference is that he did so to avoid me because he doesn't like me, which may be true or false. Inferences may be made about the future, as predictions, or about the past or present. The importance of inferences for CBC is that they are hypotheses, which means there are alternatives which may be equally true or false (described in stage 1) and they stand to be challenged (as described later), and hence open to change.

Evaluations. Inferences by themselves do not lead to emotional consequences. Even if I infer someone is avoiding me because he doesn't like me, that in itself will not bother me, unless I then go on to evaluate that being disliked by him is bad for *me* in some way. This brings us to the second type of belief the counsellor needs to identify – the evaluation. We use the term evaluation because it refers to a judgment about whether something is good or bad, desirable or undesirable, wonderful or horrible, or something in between these extremes. Drawing a negative evaluation at B does lead to a negative emotion at C. We now describe inferences and evaluations in more detail.

Inferences
An inference is a hypothesis that goes beyond the evidence. An inference implies that whenever X occurs, Y will follow. It takes a

logical form as follows: 'If X then Y. X therefore Y.' The client doesn't often see it as an inference but simply as two connected facts, X and Y. In the simplest form of the inference, A is the activating event, and B is a belief in an ABC episode, for example, 'He walked to the other side of the road' (A); 'He doesn't like me' (B). Clients commonly do not give the full inference, but may only give the A ('He walked to the other side of the road') or the B ('He doesn't like me'), but an ABC assessment will give the counsellor both halves of the inference, and she will be able to use the inference as the bridge between A and B.

One way to get at an inference is for the counsellor to first focus on a specific ABC episode, and then connect A and B in an 'If ... then ...' sentence frame. For example, a client is terrified (C) of certain throat sensations (A) and believes it means she has got cancer (B). Client inference: *if* she gets a throat sensation, *then* she has got cancer.

Inference chains. A more complex situation is where several inferences are connected in a chain. The first inference in a chain will be similar to the one above, where X is the factual part and Y goes beyond the available evidence. However, the factual part may then masquerade as a later inference. For example, a client gets depressed (C) when his girlfriend does not telephone as promised (A) and believes it means she has gone out with another man (first B inference) which means she doesn't like him any more (second B inference) which means no girl will ever like him (third B inference). Inference chain: 'If he doesn't get the call, then she has gone out with another man, and if she has gone out with another man it means she doesn't like him any more ...' etc. We will later demonstrate a full inference and evaluation chain.

It is rare for the client to be aware that his thinking takes the form of an inference, but the inference is there nonetheless and the counsellor can draw it out and make it explicit in the way described. Sometimes the client will not connect the A and B for himself, and will just simply refer to the B ('I've got cancer' or 'She doesn't like me'). But the counsellor knows the A is there – not verbalised perhaps, but assumed. She then helps the client make explicit both the fact, A, and the inference drawn from the fact, B.

Types of inferences. There are certain types of errors like the last one that commonly occur in inferences, and which it is useful for the counsellor to be aware of, so that she can recognise them and be ready to dispute them when they occur. Beck (1976) identified six such errors:

Arbitrary inference, mentioned above, refers to the process of drawing a specific conclusion quite arbitrarily. The lady with the throat sensation does this when she infers she has cancer.

Selective abstraction consists of focusing on a detail taken out of context, ignoring other more salient features of the situation and conceptualising the whole experience on the basis of this fragment. The lady with the throat sensation also does this, since there are many other stimulus events going on at the same and different times which she does not attend to.

Overgeneralisation refers to the pattern of drawing a general rule or conclusion on the basis of one or more isolated incidents and applying the conclusion to virtually all situations. The 'jilted' man does this when he assumes no girl will ever like him.

Magnification and minimisation are reflected in gross errors in evaluating the significance or magnitude of an event. The 'jilted' man does this by magnifying the meaning of the absent telephone call, and minimising the importance of the numerous occasions when friends have spontaneously rung him.

Personalisation refers to the patient's tendency to relate external events to himself. This is one form of arbitrary inference, in which the patient tends to blame himself for things that goes wrong. Another term used for this tendency is self-attribution.

Absolutistic, dichotomous thinking is the tendency to place everything into one of two opposite categories. Thus an error is a catastrophe, a failure is a complete failure. We provide examples in the next section.

Action Summary
1 The counsellor explains what an inference is, using both realistic and unrealistic examples from everyday life. She then turns to the client's A, and identifies the factual part in it.
2 The counsellor then identifies the inference, B, which is drawn from the fact.
3 The counsellor paraphrases both the fact, A, and the inferences drawn and makes a mental note of the type of error the client makes.
4 The client confirms the inference (or corrects it). The counsellor then writes down the inference in the dysfunctional B column on the ABC form.
5 The counsellor repeats steps 1 to 4 for the subsequent inferences if there is a chain, each time writing down the inferences in the dysfunctional B column.

Case Example
[The counsellor has explained what an inference is, with examples, and how to use the sentence frame if . . . then . . .]

1 *Counsellor*: Let us see if we can identify your inferences in the evening class situation. You are sitting in the classroom. Then what? What are you predicting that makes you so anxious?
  Client: That he will catch my eye.
  Counsellor: So let's assume that he does catch your eye. [*Here the inference is treated as a fact.*]
2 *Counsellor*: Then what? Supposing he catches your eye?
  Client: Then he will make me talk.
  Counsellor: So let's say your inference, B, is: 'Then he will make me talk.'
3 *Counsellor*: The full statement then is 'If he catches my eye, then he will make me talk.' Is that correct?
4 *Client*: Yes, correct.
5 *Counsellor* [*writes this inference in the dysfunctional B column.*] Right. Let's assume again that he does make you talk ... then what ...?
  Client: Then I will freeze up. Nothing will come out ... etc.

Evaluations

As we pointed out earlier, people respond emotionally at C not to activating events themselves, not even to their inferences at B, but to their *evaluations* of A or of their inferences at B. We now turn to this important task of identifying and assessing the evaluative thinking of the client.

There are a number of considerations of which the counsellor will want to be aware when she assesses client evaluations, ranging from being able to distinguish evaluations from inferences, to being able to identify the various types of dysfunctional evaluations. For example:

John walked to the other side of the street because he doesn't like me. [Inference.] I want him to like me and it's too bad that he doesn't. [First evaluation.] Not being liked by John is not just bad, it's awful. [Second evaluation.] He must like me. [Third evaluation.]

In this example we have distinguished one inference and three negative evaluations. However, it is not so much the negative evaluations themselves that lead to most of the emotional disturbance, but the gross exaggerations that people introduce into them. For example, the first evaluation ('I want him to like me and it's too bad that he doesn't') won't cause a lot of distress because the client is realistically saying that it is bad that he is not getting what he wants. But the second ('It's *awful*') and third ('He *must* like me') evaluations introduce extreme and unrealistic exaggerations that do lead to distress. Assessment of negative evaluations is mainly about uncovering these unrealistic exaggerations and distinguishing them from more realistic negative evaluations.

These considerations can be separated into a number of principles. We discuss these principles in the form of five questions which the counsellor may find it helpful to ask of the client's stated Bs.

Question 1: Is this belief an inference or an evaluation? How does the counsellor know when the client is expressing an evaluation as opposed to an inference? Inferences, as we have seen, are hypotheses about reality and can be confirmed or disconfirmed, while evaluations are assertions of value or preference and are good or bad. The counsellor knows when the client is evaluating when he talks about what he likes or dislikes, wants and doesn't want, values and does not value and what was good or bad for him. These are realistic evaluations. Unrealistic evaluations are gross exaggerations of these, and we shall show how these come about in the next four questions.

A good rule of thumb is that an inference can be confirmed or disconfirmed, whereas an evaluation is judged good or bad.

Question 2: Who is evaluating whom or what? There are four possibilities of concern to us. The client may be evaluating himself or his behaviour (self-to-self); someone else may be evaluating the client (other-to-self); the client may be evaluating someone else (self-to-other), or some*thing* else such as life events or life conditions (self-to-it). Each of these possibilities has different implications for disputing, as we shall show.

Question 3: Is a part or the whole of a person or the world being evaluated? A person may evaluate a single item of a person's behaviour or a single life event or place in the world ('That was a bad action'; 'That was a bad thing/situation'), a person's trait or role, or type of event/situation ('He is a bad teacher'; 'Interviews are bad'), or the whole of a person or the world ('He is a totally bad character'); 'The world is a bad place'). Very often a self-evaluating client may escalate from one extreme to the other, by first condemning a single action, generalising to all actions of this type, generalising again to a trait or role of which these types of actions form a part, and finally, generalising to the whole person ('I taught that class badly. I teach all my classes badly. I'm a useless teacher. I'm a complete failure.') Whole person negative evaluations are one of the most dysfunctional of all evaluations, leading to the greatest amount of disturbance. It is conversely often true that a client who is very distressed at C will be harbouring whole-person negative evaluations at B, and the counsellor should therefore probe for these.

Question 4: Is the evaluation relative or absolute? The distinction between relative and absolute is logically similar to the distinction between part and whole, but in this case we are referring to the intensity of the evaluation rather than the action or person being evaluated. We can illustrate this with the distinction between bad and awful (or terrible). An evaluation of *relative* badness can range from a little to a lot, whereas an evaluation of *absolute* badness can only mean 'awful' – that is, 100 per cent. In other words relative evaluations are always less than or more than, whereas absolute evaluations by definition are always totally one thing or another. Absolutistic thinking may be applied to a variety of evaluations:

(a) Evaluations of relative unworthiness become evaluations of total unworthiness. ('That was rather unfair. In fact it was terrible.')

(b) Evaluations of less use become evaluations of total useless-ness. ('That wasn't very good. In fact it was hopeless.') Like whole person evaluations, absolute evaluations lead to marked emotional disturbance, and the counsellor should probe for these, especially in clients showing high levels of distress.

Question 5: Is the evaluator preferring or demanding a change in the person evaluated, or preferring or demanding change in life conditions or events? The distinction between preferring and demanding is that a preference is a realistic desire for change in oneself or other people whereas a demand is an unrealistic absolutistic requirement that a change must take place. Such demands often go together with whole-person and absolute evaluations – 'I (you) must never make another mistake because it will prove that I'm (you're) a totally worthless person.' One form of demand applies to the tolerance (or lack of tolerance) of discomfort or frustration. Clients who demand less discomfort (be it pain or feelings) are much more likely to be emo-tionally disturbed than clients who prefer – no matter how strongly – less discomfort. This topic is dealt with in detail in Chapter 6.

Action Summary
As the client gives his Bs, the counsellor asks herself the following questions:

1 Is this an inference or a (negative) evaluation?
2 If an evaluation, who is making it of whom or what? If not clear, ask the client.
3 Is the evaluation applied to a person's single action or an isolated event/situation, a person's role or type of event/situation, or the person as a whole or the world as a whole? If not clear, ask the client. Probe for a whole person or a whole world evaluation if not given.
4 Is the evaluation relative or absolute? Probe for absolutes if not given.
5 Is the evaluator preferring or demanding a change in the person or life situation being evaluated? Probe for demanding thinking if not apparent.

An example of each type of negative evaluation is given in Andrew's inference and evaluation chain below.

Chaining

We have described inferences and evaluations, and described ways of identifying and assessing them. However, the client will generally report his inferences and evaluations in connected chains rather than in isolation. We shall now show how we can use these connections in a powerful technique which conceptually simplifies the counsellor's task and helps to elicit elusive beliefs. The method is known as chaining. The idea is that the client automatically and unconsciously makes a series of inferences followed by a series of evaluations which are linked in a chain to each other, culminating in emotional and behavioural consequences. By a series of Socratic questions and other counselling skills the counsellor helps the client adopt new beliefs at each step.

Although we recommend that the counsellor uses chaining, we would advise that the client be given plenty of time to report new beliefs, and to be aware that it can take some time to get a complete sequence. It is best to settle for part of a chain rather than pressurise and interrogate the client. The chain can be returned to in subsequent interviews.

The best way to explain the chain is with an example from our client, Andrew. The reader will remember that Andrew has joined an evening class but feels so frightened sitting in the class that he has a sense of being frozen and unable to move, although he also feels an urgent need to flee from the room. How does Andrew go from such an apparently innocuous activating event as sitting in the class to such a powerful fear? At first, Andrew doesn't appear to know. As far as he experiences it, he is sitting there and the fear just happens instantaneously. However, the counsellor helps him lay out a long inference and evaluation chain. We present below such a chain of beliefs, as the Bs in an ABC assessment. The type of belief, corresponding to the guidelines suggested above, is given in brackets:

Andrew's Chain

Activating event

Andrew is sitting at a desk in the middle of a crowded room at an evening class. As the teacher talks, individuals periodically put up their hands, at which point the teacher invites them to comment.

Beliefs (about A)

List of dysfunctional thoughts/images

If I sit here, *he will sooner or later catch my eye.* [Inference.]

If he catches my eye, *I will be asked to talk about something.* [Inference.]

If I'm asked to talk, *I will freeze, and nothing will come out.* [Inference.]

That would be bad. [Relative evaluation of part of self.]

People will think that's absolutely pathetic behaviour. [Inference that others will make absolute evaluation of part of self.]

And if that's what they would think, *they'd be right.* [Absolute evaluation of part of self.]

That would be awful. I would believe I was a totally pathetic and worthless person. [Absolute evaluation of whole of self.]

I absolutely have to avoid having people see me freeze up, or else I'd be shown up to be a complete idiot. I have to get out. [Demanding total avoidance of negative evaluation by others.]

Consequences (of B)

Andrew is feeling extremely anxious. His body is tense and rigid, and he is perspiring and feeling nauseous.

Note: The italicised statements are written down in sequence in the dysfunctional B column of the ABC form.

The inference and evaluation chain at B reveals clearly how Andrew apparently comes to be so distressed at C simply by sitting in the evening class at A. By means of his inferences, Andrew makes a prediction that the whole class will judge his behaviour pathetic. By means of his evaluations, he concludes that he would be worthless if this happens, and must avoid it happening at all costs. The counsellor's formulation would probably be that the underlying thread of his evaluations is a probable core belief that he must have people's respect or else he is a worthless person. We shall return to this in the closing phase.

Action Summary
The most important and difficult part of chaining is getting to the client's evaluations. The following focuses on this difficulty.

1 Get the client to state his first belief in the manner outlined in Chapter 2; for example, 'What was it about A that led you to feel so C?', or 'What was it about being asked a question that led you to feel so anxious?'

2 Repeat the client's first inference in a paraphrase, and then treat it as an A, and repeat step (1) but varying your question. For example, ask: 'What follows from that?' An alternative strategy is to tie each inference given to the emotional C with a paraphrase and question such as: 'You say you will fumble your words. How would

that make you feel so anxious?' If the client says: 'Because people will laugh at me' the counsellor says: 'And suppose, as you claim, people will laugh at you, what would you be saying to yourself to make you feel *that* anxious?' Or the counsellor can repeat the question: 'And then what?'

3 This routine is then repeated with the next inference, and the next, until the evaluations are reached.

4 Repeat the routine with the evaluations. If the client is not giving his exaggerated evaluations, use your knowledge of what the exaggeration is likely to be to frame your question. For example, 'You say it would be bad. *How* bad?' Be sure to continue probing until you get the exaggerated and demanding evaluations (if they exist).

Case Example

This example is a fragment of a chain, to show how the counsellor helps the client get to his evaluations.

> *Counsellor*: You say you would freeze and nothing would come out. [Client's inference.] What would be so anxiety-provoking in your mind about that?
> *Client*: Well, I wouldn't be giving an answer. [Inference repeated in different words.]
> *Counsellor*: And if you didn't give an answer, what then?
> *Client*: I'd want to fly out the room. [Jumps to consequence.]
> *Counsellor*: Why would you?
> *Client*: Well, people would think that was an absolutely pathetic way to behave. [Infers others would make absolute evaluation of part of self.]
> *Counsellor*: And if they did think that? . . .
> *Client*: They'd be right wouldn't they? [Absolute evaluation of part of self.]
> *Counsellor*: And if it was an absolutely pathetic way to behave, what would that mean?
> *Client*: That I'd be worthless. [Absolute evaluation of whole of self.]

Cognitive Intervention

The method of assessment we have advocated earlier means that the counsellor should now have an accurate ABC episode (or several such episodes) in which the account of A is truly relevant and factual, the account of C accurately reflects a distressing emotion and a self-defeating pattern of behaviour (or behavioural tendency), the account of B contains all the relevant beliefs and within B a careful distinction has been made between inferences and evaluations. The client will have shared in an important discrimination-learning experience, in which he will have had to decide if apparent activating events were really beliefs, whether apparent emotional consequences (like 'falling apart', 'going to pieces') were really also beliefs, and the difference between inferences and evaluations. This careful assessment makes the intervention task much easier, since the tools of intervention can now be properly targeted.

CBC intervention requires some particular skills of interviewing style which seeks to give as little direct advice to the client as possible but instead seeks to elicit solutions from the client, and in this way builds on the client's own capacity to problem-solve. This procedure, known as the Socratic method, is based around the use of open and closed questions, and is an invaluable addition to basic counselling skills. A useful account of the method is given in Beck et al. (1979).

It will now be clear that the main focus of intervention is the B, though the way to it can be not only directly through B, but indirectly through A or C, as we shall show. In stage 1 we introduced the method of alternative thinking as a way of producing change in the client's beliefs. The advantage of that method is that the client does the work and *owns* the alternatives, and this ensures that they stand a good chance of fitting into his overall construct system. However, a potential disadvantage is that the client may have insufficient faith in the alternatives compared to the strongly-held and automatic dysfunctional beliefs. The client will often automatically assume there is overwhelming evidence for his dysfunctional belief, especially if – as is usually the case – he has not thought it through or objectively sought for evidence. In such a case we need to turn to another method, called disputing, which is a way of explicitly examining all beliefs for their evidence.

Disputing Inferences

Disputing is based on the scientific method, in which hypotheses are made, and then tested in experiments for evidence that verifies or falsifies them. Hypotheses found to be true are then accepted, while those found to be false are abandoned or modified.

Disputing is a way of systematically asking: Is this belief firmly based on reality or on fantasy? If on reality, then it should be adhered to, but if based on fantasy, then it should be abandoned. The whole thrust of CBC, of course, is the claim that most client beliefs that underlie extreme forms of distress and self-defeating behaviour are not based on reality, and are therefore susceptible to the method of attack by disputing.

In order to carry out disputing, it is important to understand thoroughly what an inference is, and the reader is advised to re-read the explanation given in the last section. The main procedure for disputing inferences, described in detail below, requires the counsellor to focus on the conclusion in an identified inference and to challenge it as a B (as a hypothesis) by asking for evidence that verifies it or seeking evidence that falsifies it.

In the case of the client who is terrified (C) of certain throat sensations (A) and believes it means she has got cancer (B), the counsellor asks for the evidence that allows her to conclude from the premise that she has cancer. In the case of the client who gets depressed (C) when his girlfriend does not telephone as promised (A), the counsellor asks what evidence enables him to conclude that she has gone out with another man (first B), that she doesn't like him any more (second B), and that no girl will ever like him (third B). And in Andrew's case, what is the evidence he would be asked to talk about something, since (as it turns out) the teacher has never asked anyone to talk, only responded to requests to talk.

To summarise, the classic challenge to an inference is simply: What is the evidence? So, for example: What is the evidence that B follows from A? Or alternatively: What is the evidence that A will be followed by, lead to, or imply B? 'What is the evidence that you will get cancer if you have sensations in the throat?' 'What is the evidence that her failing to telephone means she doesn't like you etc.?' 'What is the evidence you would be asked to talk?'

The power of disputing can be increased in a number of ways. One is to seek with the client evidence that will *falsify*, rather than verify, the inference. For example, the throat sensation has existed for years, but the client is still in perfect health. The 'jilted' boyfriend can recall numerous examples when friends haven't kept to a promise, without this in any way showing they didn't like him any more. Andrew has for many years predicted that he would freeze up 'for certain' if 'put on the spot', but the evidence has always proved him wrong.

A way of disputing an arbitrary inference, for example, is to ask the client what *alternative* conclusions he might draw from the same premise. This makes effective use of the alternative thoughts method we introduced in stage 1. The client is invited to compare the evidence for the alternative conclusion with that for the first conclusion.

Sometimes it is very difficult to find any evidence for or against an inference – for example, what strangers may be thinking in the street. It is useful in a situation like this to get the client to think of at least half-a-dozen alternative inferences, and help him to see that it is quite arbitrary which of these alternatives he should believe.

One way of dealing with selective abstraction is to get the client to list a number of other stimuli or events in the same conceptual domain as the original one, especially ones which have a positive value for the client. For example, the client who focuses on a failed task at work can list the other tasks he did successfully but failed to monitor. Ways of disputing other cognitive errors and false inferences are suggested in Chapter 6.

Action Summary

1 Take the previously filled in ABC form. Starting with the first inference in the chain, ask the client what evidence he has to support or prove the inference.
2 Ask the client how the evidence provided (if any) proves the inference.
3 Steps 1 to 2 are recycled until the client agrees his inference is invalid or is modified until it is realistic, or can show that it was in fact realistic. Write down the realistic version of the inference in the second B column on the assessment form, opposite the unrealistic inference which was previously written.
4 An option is to invite the client to think of evidence which also disconfirms an invalid inference.
5 Another option is to invite the client to think of alternative conclusions for which there is better evidence, or which are as likely to be the case as his own conclusion.
6 Repeat the above steps for each of the client's inferences, writing down each new conclusion on the form.

Case Example

1 *Counsellor*: Andrew, what is the evidence that if the teacher catches your eye, he will ask you to talk?
   Client: Well, that is the kind of thing teachers do.
   Counsellor: Is that evidence, or is that a belief you have about teachers?
   Client: It's a belief, but it does happen.
2 *Counsellor*: Many things do happen, but how is that evidence that *this* teacher will ask *you* to talk in *this* situation?
   Client: Well, he does actually look around the classroom.
   Counsellor: And ask people to talk?
   Client: Er, well no. He only responds to requests.
3 *Counsellor*: So what would be a more realistic inference?
   Client: If he catches my eye, he will invite me to talk if I request it.
   Counsellor: Let's write that down.

Disputing Evaluations

Helping clients to change their invalid inferences and learning more realistic ones is a potent procedure, but still leaves the client vulnerable. Sooner or later the client will have to contend with negative evaluations, and if he has dysfunctional negative beliefs of the type

outlined in the last section, he will soon return to disturbing conclusions such as low self-worth, leading to depression or some other
distressing emotion.

To help the client achieve more long-lasting relief from his disturbance, the counsellor is strongly advised to dispute the client's dysfunctional evaluations. But which evaluations can the counsellor
dispute? In the section on assessment of evaluations, we used five
questions to group together types of evaluations that the counsellor
might identify. In this section we will follow the same procedure, in
that we will go through the five questions again and suggest where
and how to dispute. The reader will also find a comprehensive list of
dysfunctional evaluations, and methods of disputing, in Chapter 5.

The products of the disputes – a new realistic evaluation – should
be written down in the second B column of the assessment form,
opposite the appropriate disputed belief.

Question 1: Is this belief an inference or an evaluation? The
approach to disputing inferences versus evaluations is, of course,
quite different. While inferences can be disputed on the basis of
whether they can be confirmed or disconfirmed (as shown in the last
section), ordinary non-exaggerated evaluations are assertions of
good and bad, likes and dislikes, and are not disputable as such, since
people simply *have* their preferences, and do not infer them from
anything. A rule of thumb for ordinary, non-exaggerated evaluations, therefore, is simply that it is neither appropriate nor even
possible to dispute people's preferences, no matter how different
your own preferences may be.

Examples of dislikes that we would not dispute at an evaluative
level (though we might well dispute them as inferred facts) are being
less attractive, less intelligent, rejected by someone, making mistakes or failing to achieve something, or being made use of. An
example from Andrew's case is his evaluation 'That would be bad'
when referring to freezing up in front of strangers. (However, we
might dispute these evaluations if the client were turning them into
evaluations of worth. The counsellor can in that case challenge the
client to show how his strong dislike of being, for example, less
attractive than he would like, can ever prove that he is unworthy as a
person.)

If it is not advisable for the counsellor to dispute most evaluations
(that is, non-exaggerated evaluations), what does the counsellor do
to help the client get relief from the discomfort that such an evaluation might bring? The answer is that the counsellor does not help the
client get relief, but rather helps the client face up to the 'reality' of
realistic negative evaluations and the accompanying discomfort. But
as soon as the client says he cannot tolerate the discomfort (for

example, 'It is awful; I can't stand it') then the counsellor knows that the client has gone beyond an ordinary functional evaluation to a dysfunctional one – in this case, one that we discuss under question 4 below. And this brings us to a final point under question 1, for although the counsellor will not want to dispute most evaluations, she certainly will dispute the fallacies and gross exaggerations that clients introduce into their evaluations. We now examine ways of disputing these distortions (questions 2 to 5).

Question 2: Who is evaluating whom or what? In the assessment section we considered four possibilities: self-to-self, other-to-self, self-to-other and self-to-it evaluations. We will take each in turn and consider whether it is appropriate to dispute it.

Self-to-self evaluations. We have looked at the case where someone may express his dislike of some self-characteristic such as being less attractive. Self-to-self evaluations of this type referred to under question 1 would not normally be disputed, as we pointed out. However, the counsellor *would* be advised to dispute self-evaluations of the whole person such as 'I'm totally inadequate' (this is dealt with under question 3), or self-evaluations of an absolute, dogmatic kind as in 'what I did was absolutely awful' (this is dealt with under question 4) or self-evaluations that the client is demanding must be changed such as 'I mustn't make any more mistakes' (dealt with under question 5). Before definitely deciding against disputing an apparently realistic self-evaluation, the counsellor may like to satisfy herself that the client isn't implicitly also making one of these other, exaggerated evaluations or demands. For example, when Andrew says 'that would be bad' when referring to freezing up in front of others, does he mean just relatively bad, or does he really mean it would be awful?

Other-to-self evaluations. Let us suppose the client infers someone has made an evaluation that something the client did was bad, and accepts the evaluation as true simply because that person stated it, as in 'I am hopeless at dealing with my children – my Mother told me so'. This common belief is disputed on the grounds that saying something is the case doesn't make it the case. There are a number of analogies that make this simple but powerful logical point clear to the client. One is the Unicorn technique – the counsellor asserts the client is a Unicorn, using the client's logic to substantiate the claim. The client then has to imagine a 'powerful' other, such as a domineering mother, making the same assertion. For example:

Client: If people thought that freezing and drying up was pathetic they'd be right.
Counsellor: How does that follow?

Client: Well, you've got to accept what people think of you – that's facing up to reality.
Counsellor: Is it? Supposing I think you are a Unicorn, would you become one?
Client: No of course not.
Counsellor: But supposing someone whose opinion you respect very much – such as your mother – said you were a Unicorn. Would you be one then?
Client: No, that's ridiculous.
Counsellor: So it clearly doesn't follow that you become what people think you are. Can you think of a more realistic alternative belief to that one?
Client: Calling someone names doesn't change them.

The counsellor should also attend to the type of evaluation that the other is said to be making of the client. Is it an evaluation about a part or the whole of the client (see question 3), or a relative or absolute evaluation (see question 4), or an evaluation in which the other is preferring or demanding some change in the client (see question 5). Each of these kinds of evaluations can then be disputed as suggested in the guidelines below.

Self-to-other evaluations. Imagine this time that the client makes an evaluation that something someone *else* did was bad, and accepts that this is true of the other simply because the client believes it. Needless to say, this belief is disputable in much the same way as other-to-self evaluations are disputable. In other words, the client's believing something is the case doesn't make it the case. The other person doesn't become bad just because the client believes or states this.

Self-to-it evaluations. The logic of disputes of self-to-it evaluations is the same as that for other-to-self and self-to-other evaluations. For example, if a client evaluates 'modern' life as bad compared to the 'old times' this should not be viewed as an objective feature about 'modern' life but as a subjective evaluation of the client's.

Question 3: Is a part or the whole of the person being evaluated? A self-to-self evaluation of a particular behaviour is not usually disputable, unless the evaluation is being exaggerated in the way described in question 4. However, any kind of evaluation of the whole of a person is always disputable. There are two reasons for this: one is that human beings never conform to single labels but are complex, free agents who may at any time behave in unpredicted ways. The second is that human beings are both fallible and worthwhile. One of the clearest leads here is given by Albert Ellis (for example, Ellis and Dryden, 1987) which is to endorse the principle that human beings are intrinsically worthwhile even though they are also intrinsically fallible, which means that people can rightly condemn their bad behaviour but not their whole self. The rule of thumb here is that

negative evaluations of 'parts' of a person, for example, single behaviours or traits or roles may be true, but evaluations of the whole
can never be true. The counsellor bases her challenge on the request
for evidence that the individual totally conforms to one evaluation, or
a request for evidence that a bad act makes a bad person. Further
guidance on this type of dispute is given in Chapter 5.

Question 4: Is the evaluation relative or absolute? As we pointed out
earlier, here the emphasis is on the intensity of the evaluation,
whereas in question 3 the focus was on the person evaluated. Many
people believe they are not attractive enough, but vary in how bad
they judge this – some believing it is quite bad, others judging it very
bad (meaning they dislike it a lot). These are all evaluations of
relative badness, and are subjective opinions which we cannot objectively dispute, though we may disagree. However, if the client makes
a dogmatic evaluation that his lack of attractiveness is absolutely bad,
that is, awful, then the counsellor will usually want to dispute this.
The basis of disputing is similar to, and equally as powerful as, the
basis of disputing in question 3, namely that there can be no possible
evidence for an absolute evaluation. The basis of this dispute is that
'absolutes' do not exist in the real world. For example, absolute 100
per cent badness means nothing could be worse, whereas in the real
world we can always produce a worse example. The best way to use
this dispute is not to try to justify to the client that most things are
relative, but rather to challenge the client for evidence to support his
absolutising. The counsellor can help the client realise that there is no
possible evidence to support absolute claims.

The two forms of exaggeration discussed under questions 3 and 4 –
whole person evaluations and absolute evaluations – do not necessarily go together – I might believe I did a terrible thing without
believing I'm a terrible person. But sometimes they do go together,
and the counsellor is advised to be on the lookout particularly for
their co-occurrence, as in this example with our client Andrew:

Client: Freezing up in front of others would be awful. I would feel I was a
  totally useless person.
Counsellor: Can I just clarify what you mean there. By a totally useless
  person, do you mean a person who is absolutely, completely useless at
  absolutely everything, always has been and always will be?
Client: Er, yes.
Counsellor: Can you tell me how that could happen?
Client: Well, take this problem – if I froze up . . .
Counsellor: And that would prove it?
Client: I suppose not. I'm exaggerating.
Counsellor: Perhaps you are exaggerating about awful too, since awful
  means it couldn't possibly be worse.
Client: But I do mess up a lot of things and they *are* pretty bad.

Counsellor: So you are fallible. I'm sure you can live with that. I can!
Client: I see the point.
Counsellor: Can you think of a realistic evaluation?
Client: I'm not totally useless – I just make mistakes sometimes and that's unfortunate.

Question 5: Is the evaluator preferring or demanding a change in the person evaluated or the event/situation/life conditions, etc. being evaluated? The counsellor does not dispute a client's preference for change in himself or others, or a preference for situations to be different, since preferences – no matter how strongly expressed – allow for real-world disappointments. However, it is generally advisable for the counsellor to dispute a client's *demands* for changes or for situations to be different. There are three main types of dispute for demands. One is similar to the dispute for absolute evaluations, namely that it is unrealistic (not to say pointless) to demand that the world – and principally people – are different from the way they are. The second is that people are fallible by their natures and cannot be made to perform infallibly, which the demand requires.

The third approach to demands is to undermine the motive for making them, by showing the client that the motive for making them is to avoid the terrible consequence of utter catastrophe and devastating worthlessness – neither of which exist, as shown by previous disputes. These disputes are illustrated in the following example:

Client: I must avoid any possibility of drying up at all costs.
Counsellor: Why *must* you avoid it?
Client: I'd die if it happened.
Counsellor: If that were true (and we are disputing that) that would be a good reason why you must definitely and very strongly *want* to avoid it. But why *must* you avoid it?
Client: Because I'd hate it.
Counsellor: But that's more evidence for strongly preferring to avoid it happening, but no evidence for why it must not happen.
Client: But the consequences are so bad, that's why.
Counsellor: Bad things happen all the time. We cannot demand that they don't.
Counsellor: What's a better alternative?
Client: I don't like freezing up in front of others. I will try very hard to avoid it, but I realise I don't *have* to avoid it. It's bad but not terrible.

Action Summary
1 Counsellor and client move from the inferences to the evaluations on the ABC form.
2 The counsellor gets the client to imagine that events turn out the way he inferred (being careful to remind the client that the evidence is probably against such an outcome), and then to think about the core evaluations.

3 The counsellor disputes the evaluation if this is relevant, in accordance with our suggestions in questions 1 to 5.

4 The counsellor then invites the client to think of an alternative, non-exaggerated evaluation, and writes this down in the dysfunctional B column on the assessment form.

Chaining and Disputing

The full power of disputing comes not in challenging isolated beliefs, but of challenging whole chains of inferences and evaluations, producing a cumulative undermining of the client's conclusions. Let us reconsider Andrew's chain presented in the last section, and the alternative chain of more helpful, realistic inferences and evaluations that emerged in this section:

Andrew's Chain

Activating event

Andrew is sitting at a desk in the middle of a crowded room at an evening class. As the teacher talks, individuals periodically put up their hands, at which point the teacher invites them to comment.

Beliefs (about A)

Dysfunctional chain	*Functional chain*
If I sit here, *he will sooner or later catch my eye.* [Unrealistic inference.]	If I sit here, *he may sooner or later catch my eye if I try to attract his attention.*
If he catches my eye, *I will be asked to talk about something.* [Unrealistic inference.]	If he catches my eye, *he may invite me to talk if I request it.*
If I'm asked to talk *I will freeze and nothing will come out.* [Unrealistic inference.]	If I'm asked to talk (very unlikely), *I may freeze, though it has never happened yet. On the evidence, I am much more likely not to freeze.*
That would be bad. [Relative evaluation of part of self.]	If I did freeze up (very unlikely), *I wouldn't like it.*
People will think that's absolutely pathetic behaviour. [Infers others will make absolute evaluation of part of self.]	If I freeze up (very unlikely), *some people might think that's pathetic behaviour, but then different people are likely to think all sorts of different things.*
And if that's what they would think, *they would be right.* [Absolute evaluation of part of self.]	Even if some people thought it was pathetic behaviour, *that wouldn't make it pathetic. Calling someone names doesn't change them.*

Beliefs (about A)

Dysfunctional chain	*Functional chain*
That would be awful. I would believe I was a totally pathetic and worthless person. [Absolute evaluation of whole of self.]	*I could not ever be rendered a totally worthless person – just a person who makes mistakes and gets things wrong sometimes.*
I absolutely have to avoid having people see me freeze up or else I'd be shown up to be a complete idiot. I have to get out. [Demanding total avoidance of negative evaluation of whole of self.]	*I wouldn't like it, but I'd certainly survive freezing up in front of others, though I shall always try to avoid it happening.*

Consequences (of B)

Consequences of dysfunctional chain	*Consequences of functional chain*
Andrew is feeling extremely anxious. His body is tense and rigid, and he is perspiring. He is in a state of readiness to flee from the situation.	Andrew is experiencing only mild concern, because he believes the event is very unlikely, and even if it did happen, it would only show that he was fallible, not worthless.

Note: The italicised statements are written down in the B columns of the ABC form.

In this ABC episode, for the A event to be followed by C the client has to believe all the statements in the left column to be true. The counsellor knows, however, that most of those statements are probably or certainly untrue. The inferences are possible but highly improbable, and the evaluations (apart from 'that would be bad – which in any case is more accurately expressed as 'I wouldn't like that') – are false. The counsellor can therefore pick off one after another – beginning at the top with the inferences and working down through the evaluations (the order preferred by Aaron Beck and other cognitive therapists) or beginning at the bottom with the evaluations and working up (the order preferred by Albert Ellis and other rational-emotive therapists).

This example reveals an alternative chain that has very different consequences for the client than the original chain. With such an alternative, the counsellor should be able to convince the client that the numerous assumptions he makes in the left column are at the very least debatable, and that to bring his thinking in line with reality he had better change his view of the world – in line with the second column – and thereby his emotionally distressing response to it.

CLOSING PHASE

Setting Homework Tasks

The general format for homework throughout the second stage is to select one or two main beliefs to work on in one or two types of situations. This means the counsellor must keep a clear perspective of the direction of CBC – to see the wood for the trees – and not be confused by the complexities of cognitive assessment and intervention. The counsellor will encourage the client to deal with one problem at a time, but through her formulations the counsellor should be able to identify underlying beliefs that will tie several different emotional episodes together, and could be dealt with as a problem area.

There are many ways that homework can be arranged, and the counsellor can turn to Chapter 6 as a resource for ideas on different types of homework. We suggest below one particular series of tasks which draws together the method of assessment and intervention outlined in stage 2.

Action Summary
1 Ask the client to take one of the problems that have been the focus of cognitive assessment and intervention during stage 2, and use this as the basis for a particular homework assignment.
2 With the help of the relevant ABC form, review the chain of current, dysfunctional beliefs with the client.
3 Next, review the chain of functional alternative beliefs.
4 Suggest the client learn the alternative chain as thoroughly as possible, by going over the list and learning it by rote.
5 The client is asked to rehearse the alternative chain for a period of, say, 30 minutes a day, and also shortly before going to an A situation, by way of preparation.
6 Negotiate an undertaking with the client to go into the A situation as often as possible.
7 Ask the client to select one or two of the new beliefs that he finds most compelling, and write these on a cue card (such as the back of a visiting card) and to keep this in the palm of his hand or a convenient pocket. He should look at the card to remind him of the alternative thoughts whenever his emotional C reaches a level that is distressing, or whenever he starts dysfunctional ruminations.

Case Example
1 *Counsellor*: What problem would you like to select as your homework assignment this week Andrew?
   Client: I want to give the evening class priority.
2 and 3 *Counsellor*: OK, well here we have the ABC form for that problem.

Let's go through the dysfunctional chain together first followed by the alternative chain ... etc.

4 *Counsellor*: One thing you could do with the alternative chain is to learn it by heart. Do you think that is a good idea?

Client: I can't quite see the point.

Counsellor: Well, one reason would be so that you could recall an alternative belief for any single one of the dysfunctional beliefs that came to mind.

Client: OK, I'll give it a try.

5 As above.

6 As above.

7 *Counsellor*: Of course, one problem you had with your last assignment was that you were so absorbed by your automatic thoughts that you couldn't think of any alternatives. One way round this we agreed earlier was to write some alternatives on a handy card to use to cue yourself to think differently while in the situation. How about now selecting a couple of key beliefs from the alternative chain for this purpose.

Client: One thought I'd choose would be: 'I'm not a Unicorn' to remind me that if people call me something that doesn't mean they're right.

Counsellor: Good idea. And it's an easy phrase to remember. And another one?

Client: 'I'm fallible. So are the rest of you.'

Self-Set Homework Tasks

The cognitive-behavioural counsellor's tasks include helping the client to learn to apply CBC himself to emotional episodes, as well as giving direct help. One way the counsellor can help the client learn to apply CBC is through a self-set homework task. The basis of this is straightforward enough: the client is asked to choose for himself an emotional episode that occurs during the week, and to assess it himself using the ABC form. He then tries as best he can to carry out the above steps, 1 to 7. The client is advised to adopt an experimental approach to the task. The aim isn't to get it all perfectly right, but rather to try it out and see how far he can get. The problems that this throws up can be dealt with in the next counselling session.

This concludes stage 2, and the emphasis now moves from teaching the client the cognitive-behavioural method of change, to helping the client overcome blocks to applying the method without the aid of the counsellor, in preparation for termination – the topic of stage 3.

4 Stage 3: Overcoming Blocks to Change and Independence

There are two main tasks in stage 3. The first involves overcoming blocks to change, and the second deals with termination. The two tasks are linked by the theme of independence, and they also follow in sequence. Overcoming blocks occupies the later sessions of CBC and success in this task sets up the opportunity for termination. The main focus of this stage is to prepare the client for independence from counselling.

The first task is usually to help the client who can see intellectually that his new beliefs are more realistic and more helpful than his old ones, but who is often not helped in practice by this knowledge; the same events still frequently activate his old beliefs and he still gets just as upset and responds in self-defeating ways in many situations. The aim is for the counsellor to help the client to (a) get access to upsetting and progress-blocking beliefs that remain elusive; (b) gain emotional insight – the insight that comes from the 'heart' rather than the head, and (c) overcome beliefs that fuel the client's low frustration tolerance (LFT) and lead to failure to carry out homework.

The second task – to some extent a consequence of the first – is to help the client who believes he cannot cope without the counsellor and with termination of therapy. The aim is to help him to gain a sense of independence, that is, to realise that he *can* cope on his own without the help of the counsellor. We give guidance on challenging such client beliefs and helping the client develop new beliefs that facilitate the use of termination in a productive way.

This third stage contains the following phases.

Opening Phase

This includes setting up a session agenda, allowing for discussion of pressing problems, reviewing counselling so far and the homework review.

Middle Phase

This phase concentrates on overcoming blocks to change. It includes using evocative imagery, using the formulation to get at core beliefs, using emotional insight to change core beliefs and using real-life exposure to change beliefs.

Closing Phase

This phase consolidates the aim of the middle phase by getting the client to carry out relevant homework to aid emotional insight and to overcome LFT.

Termination Phase

The last phase in CBC is aimed at identifying and disputing dependency beliefs. This phase may span more than one session.

Sooner or later the client hopefully will have developed a reasonable understanding of the principles and practice of CBC and gained experience in and benefit from its use. This point will mark the end of stage 2, and the beginning of stage 3, the main task of which is to prepare the client for independence. Stage 3 is initiated by the counsellor as soon as the client indicates by his actions that he has a reasonable grasp of CBC, and is either using the method reasonably successfully – in which case the counsellor moves straight to the termination phase – or is having difficulties applying it. In the latter case the counsellor helps the client overcome blocks to using CBC, and at the same time helps the client take over the counsellor's role of problem-solving, preparatory to termination. The opportunity and need to introduce stage 3 will usually occur during the opening phase of an interview. We give an example of how this may happen during the opening phase below. In this example we shall assume that our client is experiencing difficulties in using CBC and brings it up during the homework report.

OPENING PHASE

Session Agenda

The session agenda will by now be a familiar routine that ensures that time and attention are given to issues considered important by both client and counsellor. The client may at this point want to include his difficulties in using CBC, or the counsellor may want to include a discussion about termination.

Pressing Problems

The session agenda continues to give the client space for bringing up any kind of event which for him has urgency or seriousness, or both.

Indeed it may be under this heading that the client brings up the problem of blocks or his anxieties about termination. However, the counsellor should be wary of any 'red herrings' that the client may be using to fend off discussion of difficult issues such as these.

Review of Counselling So Far

This feedback from the client may show that the client is ready for stage 3.

Homework Report

This is the most likely heading under which material indicating a shift to stage 3 will arise. The counsellor will want to focus on difficulties which require the counsellor's intervention, and which the client may feel he is unable to resolve on his own. We find that our client Andrew has a number of such difficulties with his homework: his alternative thoughts don't help him when he gets overwhelmed with panic; he sometimes gets so confused by all the possible thoughts that he can't think of an appropriate alternative one; sometimes the alternative thoughts seem weak and unconvincing compared to his dysfunctional thoughts and do not help him for that reason; and, finally, he often cannot tolerate the discomfort of his anxiety feelings and avoids situations for that reason. Client and counsellor agree that these difficulties should be the focus of stage 3 interviews and should occupy the middle phase of those interviews.

MIDDLE PHASE

The middle phase of stage 3 interviews concentrates on helping the client to overcome blocks to change while at the same time helping him to acquire the methods of overcoming such blocks. There are a variety of problems and solutions which are dealt with more comprehensively in the chapters on intervention techniques (Chapter 5) and homework (Chapter 6). Here we confine ourselves to a few common problems which we deal with in the form of Andrew's problems. Cognitive assessment and intervention are so intertwined at this point that we shall bring them together in the following section.

Using Evocative Imagery

Clients often seem unable to think in a helpful and rational way when it comes to the 'crunch' – in the actual situation in which they feel distress. One reason may be that the new belief is unconvincing compared with the dysfunctional belief – a problem we dealt with in stage 2. Another reason is that the client has not yet gained access to relevant images or beliefs that are at the heart of the emotional problem, in which case the elusive beliefs will continue to upset the client. This often means, for example, that the client is just as anxious about going into a situation, and may even repeatedly fail to do the assignment because this unidentified belief is continuing to maintain behavioural avoidance. One way of overcoming this problem, and getting access to repressed and elusive beliefs is by vivid and evocative imagery – one of a number of vivid assessment methods, described in detail elsewhere (Dryden, 1987). We will give one example here. The counsellor can ask the client to close his eyes and imagine as vividly as possible that part of an activating event which seems to evoke the strongest emotional reaction. Such evocative imagery often stimulates the client's memory concerning his emotional reactions, or may even lead to the re-experiencing of these emotions in the session. While focusing on such images, the client can begin to gain access to cognitive processes below the level of awareness that cannot be easily reached through verbal dialogue. At this point the client can be encouraged to dispute the beliefs that he now confronts and to explore helpful alternatives.

Action Summary
1 The client describes an A in which the distressing reaction is activated but is unable to describe the relevant B. Or the client is unable to get help from a new belief probably because it is not the relevant one for the A.
2 The counsellor asks the client to 'relive' in imagination the most distressing part of the activating event, and give a commentary on his dysfunctional thoughts and images.
3 The client reports his dysfunctional thoughts and images.
4 The counsellor asks the client (or suggests) functional alternative thoughts (after disputing if necessary) and suggests that the client uses the new thought in his next assignment.

Case Example
1 *Counsellor*: You say the problem about going into restaurants is even worse because you can't even go in now?
   Client: Yes. I found that writing key thoughts on a card did remind me to think the alternative thought, but the alternative thought didn't help. I still got overwhelmed with panic.
2 *Counsellor*: Let's try to use your imagination to get at the part of the situation that you are most panicked about. Can you close your eyes now and imagine being in the restaurant, and feel a full-blown panic is coming on. What's happening?

3 *Client*: People are looking at me. Oh I really don't like this. Oh no. I feel sick ... I'm being sick. It's terrible. What a disgrace. What a vile creature. What a disgusting worm. This is it, then. This is what I'm afraid of.

4 *Counsellor*: That's right. You've uncovered some unconscious thoughts and images that were troubling you. Now can you think of an alternative belief to counter *that*?

   Client: Well, I suppose anyone can be sick. Nobody likes it, but I would get over it.

   Counsellor: And what about what other people will think?

   Client: They certainly won't like it, and they may think I'm terrible. But I can live with that too. After all, it could happen to them, and no-one would condemn them.

   Counsellor: So now we have the worst that can happen. How can we use these countering thoughts to help you in the situation?

   Client: I think if I write these thoughts on a card they will be more powerful than the other ones I was trying to use.

Using the Formulation to Get at Core Beliefs

Sometimes the client is so confused by a multiplicity of thoughts in a variety of emotional episodes that he cannot easily and quickly think of a more helpful alternative. As a result he may focus on a belief which is peripheral, rather than central, to his dysfunctional way of thinking. This is where the counsellor can use a formulation, described in stage 1, to help herself and the client to identify a single, core belief that underlies a number of emotional episodes. A core belief usually takes the form of a universal rule for living such as 'I *must* succeed in virtually everything I do or else I am a worthless human being.' Such a core belief generates numerous subsidiary beliefs in specific situations such as 'I *must* win this game', or 'How terrible I made a mistake in that report.' The counsellor takes several emotional episodes that she believes cluster together and helps the client to discover the core belief that lies behind them. The client can then dispute the one core belief.

Action Summary

1 Suggest the client might have an underlying core belief which he could learn to dispute and then counter.

2 From your formulation, list several problems that you believe have a single underlying core belief.

3 Ask the client what his hunch is about what such a belief might be.

4 Suggest your own hunch, and if you agree, get the client to dispute it and write a new countering belief for use in those situations.

Case Example

> *Counsellor*: You say you are so confused by all the possible new beliefs that you can't think of a good countering thought when you're in the situation.
> *Client*: Yes, especially in the evening class.
> 1 *Counsellor*: I think it might help you to discover that there is probably only one basic belief underlying several thoughts in several activating situations.
> 2 *Counsellor*: Let's take several recent problems. [*The counsellor then lists the restaurant situation, the evening class situation, the event at work when he made a mistake in a report, and the time he felt tense playing snooker.*]
> 3 *Counsellor*: I believe all these situations have something in common for you. What are you afraid of in each one of them?
> *Client*: Well, they're all situations in which I'm worried about being thought to be stupid.
> *Counsellor*: And why are you worried about that?
> *Client*: Well, I just feel like nothing if people think I'm stupid.
> 4 *Counsellor*: Suppose you had a core belief: 'I must have virtually everyone's approval in order to be worthwhile.' Would that ring true?
> *Client*: Yes, that seems to ring true. That might be what it comes down to.
> *Counsellor*: Maybe you could dispute that core belief and find an alternative belief on that one theme. You could then apply it to all those situations . . .

Using Emotional Insight to Change Core Beliefs

Clients may report that they have clear insight into the validity of their new, functional beliefs when they feel safe and calm, and will rehearse them consistently, but these beliefs are neither convincing nor helpful when they are upset. In other words, they have intellectual insight but not emotional insight. During an emotional episode when they are depressed or anxious about something, clients may say they cannot change the way they think, either because they cannot bring to mind alternative thoughts, or they don't believe the alternative thoughts. In the latter case, their helpless, hopeless and self-condemning beliefs seem so strong and compelling that the alternatives seem weak and unconvincing in comparison, and do not stand a chance of influencing the way they feel and behave. From these clinical considerations and from the published research, the following points show why clients may not have emotional insight into their core beliefs. (We take depression as an example, but the points apply to other strong dysfunctional emotions.)

First, a client may not know what he thinks when he is depressed, until he gets depressed again. Secondly, he may not be able to get into his depressive thinking pattern, without *actually* getting depressed. Thirdly, he may learn to think functionally when he is not depressed, but he will continue to think dysfunctionally when he is depressed. Fourthly, he will not be able to 'plug in' more functional thoughts when he next gets depressed, because his existing depressogenic pattern of thinking is too strong to dislodge in that way. Depressive thinking (when depressed) is powerful, persuasive, vivid, repetitive, well-established and self-fulfilling, whereas functional thinking may be new, weak, unconvincing, and quickly abandoned and forgotten. It is sometimes rather like plugging in one cassette or computer programme at one time, another at another time, but without there being much, if any, influence between the two. The analogy is that no matter how rational a client's thinking is, it will not transfer across from a non-depressed to a depressed state – the two 'programmes' are entirely separate. The client has to be in the depressed 'programme' to learn to incorporate new thinking within it. There are two components to the procedure we suggest for gaining and using emotional insight – re-experiencing an emotional episode and mood induction.

Re-experiencing an Emotional Episode
The first approach is based on the principle of having the client re-experience one of his emotional episodes. One way of doing this is to get the client to expose himself to the A event of a particular ABC episode, with the intention of invoking the rest of the emotional episode, namely negatively exaggerated evaluative beliefs at B and consequent emotional distress at C, just as we suggested in the imaginal assessment procedure earlier. As we saw, the client is much more likely now to be able to retrieve the actual, elusive dysfunctional thoughts that give rise to his distress (rather than ones he supposes he might have), but at the same time, he is also more likely to be able to make use of the realistic, alternative thoughts, and in the very act of using those alternative thoughts, to experience emotional relief.

A Mood Induction Procedure
The counsellor should preferably be with the client throughout a re-experiencing episode during which a dysphoric mood is induced, both to ensure the client uncovers all the relevant beliefs, and also to ensure that the client actively uses countering thoughts to bring him safely out of his dysphoric mood. One of the most powerful methods of getting the client to re-experience an emotional episode actually in the counsellor's office is a 'mood induction procedure' devised by Gilbert (1986). The basic procedure builds on the chaining procedure, with which the reader will already be familiar from stage 2. The main difference from chaining, as will be shown, is that it is carried through to completion without a break, and it works mainly by literally inducing the distressing emotion.

The procedure lends itself most easily to depressive episodes. It begins with the counsellor obtaining an ABC assessment of an emotional episode, using the ABC form. She starts by obtaining the client's C and A. She asks the client to rate the intensity of the C from 0 to 100 where 100 is the worst possible. She then starts to probe for the Bs in the usual way, asking the client after each B: 'What follows from that?' or 'What thought follows next?' After each thought is elicited the counsellor asks the client to rate on a 0 to 100 scale the credibility of the belief. The counsellor takes the client down the inference and evaluation chain. As the client goes down the chain, he will inevitably become more depressed as he confronts self-condemning evaluations. The counsellor keeps a record of each inference and evaluation on the ABC form.

Once the counsellor considers that she has elicited the major evaluative beliefs, she asks the client to re-rate the intensity of the C. She then suggests to the client that they return to the top of the chain, and consider an alternative belief for each of those listed in the chain, rating each alternative belief for credibility. By this stage of CBC the client should be quite familiar with the alternative thinking procedure and with the philosophy of disputing, and should have developed some sort of repertoire of realistic alternative beliefs, with a fair degree of credibility.

The client then creates an alternative thought for each original (dysfunctional) thought in the chain, and the counsellor writes each of these down opposite the original thought, as with the chaining procedure described earlier. When they reach the bottom of the list, the client re-rates for a third time the intensity of the emotional C.

By the time the client reaches the bottom of the list (that is, the most potent evaluative thoughts) he may have considerably weakened the credibility of the dysfunctional chain and strengthened the credibility of the functional chain. The client may therefore be coming out of his dysphoric mood – as reflected in his mood rating – and may now be able to realise that he can successfully import realistic thinking into his depressive mood state, and get what we are calling 'emotional insight', that is, insight *during* that particular emotional state.

The above mood induction procedure usually has a powerful and persuasive effect on the client. He experiences, perhaps for the first time, an alternative view of himself and his situation while actually depressed, and discovers that this alternative view will change his mood state. The impossible now becomes possible for the client – to be able to modify his mood state by alternative thinking. This overcomes one of the most fundamental dysfunctional beliefs that clients have – one of helplessness to change how they feel. It proves that the alternative beliefs do work, and that they can have a strong rather than a weak effect compared to the dysfunctional beliefs.

The mood induction procedure will be of limited value, however, if the client does not use it to tackle his everyday difficulties. The client is therefore urged to carry out the procedure on his own as a homework assignment at home, by first vividly recalling an A event, inducing a depressed or anxious mood by going down the chain of thoughts, and then countering each thought, with the aid of the list on his ABC form. The client is also urged to use the procedure whenever he spontaneously feels depressed or anxious.

The counsellor may choose to use the mood induction routine on its own in the interview, as described above. But a useful technique to use after this mood induction routine is rational-emotive imagery (REI), described in Chapter 5. In REI the client is asked to imagine again as vividly as possible the A event and to state how he feels at C. He is then asked to report his most disturbing beliefs that are giving rise to the upset feeling. It should be easy for the client now to recall this belief, having just completed the mood induction routine, and he has the list of beliefs in front of him on the ABC form. The client is now asked to change his feeling, from a dysfunctional feeling (such as depression) to a functional feeling (such as strong disappointment). Having got the functional feeling firmly in mind, the client is now asked to say what he is thinking to make himself feel that way. Putting both procedures together helps to consolidate the insights, and REI gives the client a technique that is easy to remember and use.

Action Summary

1 Get the C and A of one of the client's emotional episodes, and write them down on an ABC form.
2 Start to get the first B with the question 'What thoughts come to mind when you think about A?' Write the first thought down under B (dysfunctional column). Ask the client to rate the credibility of the thought (0–100).
3 Probe for the next thought in the chain with the question ' . . . and what follows from that?' Write the second thought down, together with the credibility rating.
4 Repeat steps 2 and 3 and stop when you have at least two of the client's main evaluative beliefs.
5 Ask the client to rate the intensity of his emotional C at this moment (0–100).
6 Return to the first thought in the chain and ask the client what alternative thought or belief he might have. Write this down (alternative column), again with the credibility rating. Obtain a

second or third alternative, or suggest an alternative, if the first seems unrealistic or irrelevant.

7 Repeat step 6 for all the remaining dysfunctional thoughts, again with credibility ratings.

8 Ask the client now to re-rate the intensity of his emotional C.

Case Example

1 [*The A is that people mill around chatting to each other at work but don't chat to him. The C is feeling depressed and being very withdrawn.*]

2 *Counsellor*: What thoughts come to mind when you think about that situation?
   Client: I just can't seem to get on with people like everyone else?
   Counsellor: [*Writes thought down under B.*] How much do you think that thought is true? Give me a rating somewhere between 0 (no credibility at all) and 100 (totally credible).
   Client: 80.

3 *Counsellor*: What follows in your mind from that thought?
   Client: If I wasn't such an inadequate person, people would treat me as one of them. [*Gives rating of 80.*]

4 *Counsellor*: What thought follows from that?
   Client: I am useless because people don't respect me. [*Gives rating of 90.*]
   Counsellor: What thought follows from that?
   Client: People don't like me because they don't respect me. [*90.*]
   Counsellor: And what follows from that in your mind?
   Client: I am sure they think I am a useless slob. [*90.*]
   Counsellor: What follows next?
   Client: I suppose I am. I feel totally and completely worthless. [*100.*]

5 *Counsellor*: How do you feel now?
   Client: Terribly depressed. 100 per cent.

6 *Counsellor*: Let's return to the first thought again. Can you think of any evidence which would suggest you can get on with people?
   Client: I suppose I do get on with the boss's secretary. I don't have rows – others do. And I have my two best friends. [*Credibility rating 70.*]

7 *Counsellor*: [*Writes these ideas down.*] Can you think of any reason, other than 'inadequacy' why some people may not treat you 'as one of them'?
   Client: I suppose it could be because I don't engage in small talk. [*80.*]
   Counsellor: OK. Can you now think of any evidence against the idea that people don't respect you?
   Client: Actually people do come to me to sort out technical problems with work. I suppose they need to have some respect to do that. [*70.*]
   Counsellor: You then said they can't like you because they don't respect you.
   Client: I suppose they must like me a bit. [*70.*]
   Counsellor: And your last two statements were they must think you're a slob and they are probably right.
   Client: I suppose they can't think that if they come to me with their problems. In any case what they think doesn't prove a lot. [*90.*]

8 *Counsellor*: How do you feel now?
   Client: Like a weight has been lifted! It's down to about 20 per cent.

Client and counsellor may now reinforce the effectiveness of the induction routine by the use of rational-emotive imagery as outlined in the text above.

Using Real-Life Exposure to Change Beliefs

The mood induction procedure will not, by itself, necessarily help the client *use* his new, realistic beliefs at the time when he actually gets emotionally distressed. Suppose that the client still studiously avoids the very situations that activate the dysfunctional beliefs? The counsellor knows that what is required is that the client expose himself to the relevant activating events – not to gain insight into his underlying beliefs this time, but to use his alternative beliefs where they really matter. For example, the client who feels totally ashamed if criticised by others needs to seek out, not simply exposure to people generally but exposure to situations where he will be criticised, in order to dispute his self-condemnatory beliefs and adopt his new self-accepting beliefs. Rational-emotive therapists call this a shame-attacking exercise, and a number of exercises of this type are explored in Chapter 5.

Why is it necessary for the client to expose himself to actual criticism in the above example, rather than simply to increase his exposure to people in general? It is important for the client to have the actual *experiences* of disputing his shame-inducing belief in the context of the feared event. It is only in this way that he will gain emotional insight, rather than simply intellectual insight into his new belief: 'If people criticise me, I can still accept myself.'

Disputing LFT Beliefs to Facilitate Exposure

How can the client be helped to carry out a difficult task like this? One way is to tackle the individual's Low Frustration Tolerance (LFT), discussed in Chapter 6. According to rational-emotive theory, LFT is based on the false idea: 'Life must be easy and go the way I want. If not, it's awful and I can't stand it.' The reader will see that LFT is a further type of demanding which we referred to as one of the evaluations in stage 2. One consequence of LFT thinking is that doing any task that one is anxious about becomes not just difficult but impossible: 'I can't go into that situation. I would feel anxious. I must not feel anxious. It would be terrible. I couldn't stand it'. The belief, therefore, amplifies the experienced or anticipated intensity of the emotion, but means that in CBC we can work on reducing the client's experienced emotional intensity by disputing the LFT ideas. Such a reduction then makes it easier for the client to undertake exposure tasks of the type we have been talking about.

Action Summary

1 Suggest a shame attacking homework exercise to the client, with the rationale for changing dysfunctional beliefs.
2 If the client responds with a 'cannot', explore this as a further dysfunctional belief of the LFT type.
3 Help the client dispute the belief and replace it with a realistic alternative.
4 Explore with the client how to use the new belief to help him carry out his shame attacking exercise.

Case Example

1 *Counsellor*: So, Andrew, you have successfully disputed and abandoned the idea that you'd be a totally useless person if you froze up in front of the evening class. And you now have the helpful belief 'it could only show I'm fallible'. What could you do to put that belief to the test?
   Client: Put my hand up, get the teacher's attention and try to ask a question.
   Counsellor: Terrific idea! Will you do that?
2 *Client*: No. Sorry. It's a good idea in theory but I just couldn't do it.
   Counsellor: Let's take a look at that. Why couldn't you?
   Client: I'd panic! At the very thought my heart pounds like mad. I feel sick. It's awful. I couldn't stand it!
   Counsellor: Think about what you've learned. Where's the evidence you couldn't stand it? How could it be awful?
3 *Client*: OK, I get the point – tell myself I can stand it but it's going to be damned difficult. But I don't know that I could use that idea.
4 *Counsellor*: Don't you? How *could* you use that idea to help you do the exercise.
   Client: Hm. I suppose right at the moment I start to panic.

CLOSING PHASE

Homework

The closing phase will focus on homework assignments, which in turn will focus on the client learning ways of overcoming the remaining blocks to his applying CBC. Practical guidelines for setting homework assignments are given in chapter 6. These guidelines can be applied to the areas that we have discussed in this chapter, namely:

1 Practising vivid assessment methods such as evocative imagery to gain access to elusive beliefs.
2 Identifying and learning core beliefs, and using countering beliefs to these in relevant situations.
3 Practising mood induction procedures in order to deepen emotional insight, and bring new thinking into more effective use to produce emotional change.

4 Practising shame-attacking exercises and risk-taking exercises, and using LFT methods to change beliefs that relate to low tolerance levels, thus improving the likelihood that clients will carry out such exercises.

TERMINATION PHASE

At some point in stage 3, when the counsellor considers that the client has made some reasonable progress in overcoming his blocks to change, the counsellor will want to raise the question of termination. This is a difficult task and needs sensitive handling.

The main error the counsellor seeks to avoid is suddenly springing termination on the client (that is, in the last session), since this can lead the client to feel frightened and abandoned, even betrayed. The counsellor's goal is to use CBC as a method of helping the client to accept that he is not dependent on the counsellor for help and support, and that he can depend upon his own problem-solving capabilities, and can draw on significant others in his life – present and potential for guidance, affection and support. This task takes time and needs to be carefully planned several sessions before the end.

The counsellor will already have set the scene for terminating counselling when she negotiated the boundary conditions in stage 1. The counsellor can now reintroduce the topic of termination by reminding the client of the original agreement about number of sessions, and pointing out where they have now got to. Setting limits should not, of course, be done rigidly, but some degree of boundary-setting means the problem of termination can be tackled in a planned way. The remaining two or three sessions can then become sharply and constructively focused on helping the client to accept his independence.

Identifying and Disputing Dependency Beliefs

The most common concern that clients have about termination is that they will not be able to cope without the counsellor. Within that concern is the idea that they will not be able to make CBC work for them to solve their problems, and the other is the idea that they need the counsellor for her caring and moral support. These, and any other concerns similarly related to termination, are treated as disputable beliefs, just like any other beliefs.

The counsellor's task is to help the client realise that his termination concerns are themselves simply disputable beliefs, and to help him undertake the necessary challenging and countering. First, he looks for evidence against the prediction that he will not be able to cope, by reviewing how he has so far coped, with specific examples from the counselling to date. Secondly, she challenges the belief that he *needs* (defined as *must have* in order to be happy) the counsellor's continuing expertise, caring and moral support, rather than simply 'strongly prefers'. A way of challenging both beliefs would be by conducting an experiment, in which the client does not see the counsellor for the next four weeks, and then assesses whether he has coped or not. In Andrew's case, this last strategy is the one the counsellor adopts:

Case Example

  Client: I am not ready for termination yet. I cannot cope.
  Counsellor: Shall we have a look at the reasons why you believe you cannot cope? What reason comes first to mind?
  Client: I know I would go back to square one on my own.
  Counsellor: That sounds like a belief – a negative prediction. Perhaps we should see if that is any evidence for that.
  Client: I suppose that in terms of evidence I have had some successes in counselling. [*Gives a couple of examples.*] But it isn't going to be easy.
  Counsellor: It seems to me there is evidence for *that* belief – it isn't going to be easy. Can you live with that degree of difficulty?
  Client: I'm not sure. I still don't think I'll be able to cope on my own.
  Counsellor: Well, one thing we can do is conduct an experiment over the next four weeks . . . [*Suggests a period of separation to test the 'I can't cope' hypothesis.*]
  Client: How will that help?
  Counsellor: Well, at the moment you have the belief you cannot cope without counselling. At the end of four weeks we will be able to see if that was shown to be true or false. What do you think?
  Client: I don't like it but I see the point.

Another way the counsellor can challenge the 'I can't cope' hypothesis is to get the client to think back to his life before counselling and ask if he had coped then.

  Client: No I wasn't able to cope at all.
  Counsellor: You say that, but you were working, had a reasonable salary, a car, a flat of your own and so on.
  Client: But I didn't feel I was coping.
  Counsellor: But were you?

Similar approaches can be adopted to deal with client beliefs such as 'I must go on seeing you', 'I need to go on seeing you', 'I will feel terrible', and so on. The main aim in every case is to help the client challenge unrealistic, dependency-generating beliefs such as lack of capability, weakness, unworthiness, and to replace these with evidence-based, independence-generating beliefs which show abilities, strengths and self-worth.

At some point during these interventions the counsellor will want to make the termination of counselling definite, either by agreeing a definite date, or agreeing to decrease the frequency of sessions over time, or both. Termination should not be delayed until the client has solved all his difficulties, but should occur when the client believes he can (with difficulty) tackle his further problems independently of the counsellor. The counsellor can help the client prepare for this by anticipating future problems and working out how best to use CBC to deal with those problems. It is advisable to schedule follow-up sessions to monitor client progress in such tasks.

We have now come to the end of the complete CBC course constructed around an illustrative case. Of course, every case is different, and our case study can be no more than suggestive as to how the counsellor might proceed. The next two chapters provide more general guidelines and resource material on methods of intervention and homework setting. The final three chapters show how CBC can be applied to particular *types* of emotional disturbance.

PART II   RESOURCES

Part 1 followed the steps of CBC with one client, from the beginning to the end of counselling. Although these chapters described the main methods of creating change in a client's self-defeating thinking, the chapters could not provide a description of the full range of change-methods. In Part II an attempt is made to give a broader overview of two key areas of CBC: methods of challenging maladaptive thinking, and the use of homework tasks. The following two chapters can therefore be used for reference purposes.

Chapter 5 contains a summary of cognitive, imaginal and behavioural methods of changing a client's maladaptive thinking, and this summary includes the methods depicted in Part I, together with additional methods.

Chapter 6 is devoted to the use of homework tasks, and describes in detail how homework tasks can be designed. Success in CBC depends on the client putting into practice what is learned in counselling sessions, and therefore it is critical for clients to carry out tasks between counselling sessions.

5 An Overview of Strategies for Facilitating Change

Once the client is aware of the negative thinking which leads to a particular emotional disturbance, the counsellor can help the client to modify this thinking by means of the following procedures which were described in Chapter 3:

1 Show the client how the belief (B) leads to emotional and behavioural consequences (C).
2 Check the client's motivation to change the emotional disturbance and behaviour at C.
3 Show the client how thinking in a more realistic way at B would lead to a reduction in disturbed emotions and behaviour at C.
4 Help the client to weigh up the evidence for and against B.
5 Help the client to generate more realistic alternatives to B.

There are three main categories of strategies to modify negative thinking at points 4 and 5 of this procedure: verbal, imaginal and behavioural strategies. In a similar way to the testing of scientific hypotheses, a belief can be verified by evaluating the available evidence relating to that belief. Evidence concerning the validity of the belief can be gathered from the client's knowledge and previous experience (verbal and imaginal disputing) or by means of behavioural experiments (behavioural disputing). The counsellor may then use these various strategies to challenge the client's *inferences* about what has happened in a situation, or to challenge the client's *evaluations* about what has happened (see Chapter 3 for the distinction between inferences and evaluations).

Verbal Methods of Modifying Maladaptive Thinking

Use of Questions
Questions are the most useful tool in challenging maladaptive thinking. Rather than telling clients the realistic alternatives to their negative thoughts, it is more effective to elicit realistic thinking by means of questioning. When he is asked a series of careful questions, the client has to think through the issues involved and generate his own alternatives to negative thinking. The client will find this more convincing than being told what to think.

The form which questions take is also important. It is best to try to avoid 'why' questions as these are hard for clients to answer, and clients tend to answer 'why' questions with 'I don't know'. 'How' and 'what' questions are usually more productive. So, for example,

not, 'Why were you anxious?'

but, 'What was it about the situation which made you anxious?'

Below are some examples of the sorts of questions that are useful when disputing negative thinking:

'What's the evidence that ...?'
'How does it follow that ...?'
'What makes that terrible?'
'How do you know that?'
'Who says you must?'
'What would it take to convince you that ...?'
'What is the very worst that could happen?'
'And if that were the case?'
'How does that mean that ...?'
'What does it say about you if ...?'
'Is that something you want or an absolute need?'

In whatever way questions are phrased they will be difficult for the client to answer, and it is therefore important to leave adequate time for the client to reply. Inexperienced counsellors are inclined to ask questions too rapidly or to ask more than one question at a time. If the client provides answers which do not follow from the question, repeat the question, and if this happens persistently it would be worthwhile pointing this out to the client.

Sometimes when a counsellor questions a client's negative thoughts, the client will give a realistic line of reasoning which would not account for the way he feels. An example is the client who is anxious in case he offends people, yet who says that he is not bothered very much about what other people think about him. When a client does give a rational line of reasoning to explain a disturbed emotion, the counsellor should not be put off by this; instead she should point out to the client that he would not feel so upset if his rational response was in fact what he believed. Following the same example, the counsellor would point out that if the client were truly not bothered that much about other people's opinions about him, he would not be so worried about causing offence.

In addition to questioning, there are a number of other strategies which can be used to help the client to evaluate the evidence for his beliefs, and the logicality of his thinking. These methods include information-giving, use of analogies, humour, modelling and role reversal.

Information-Giving

Explanations and information can be helpful when the client has a misconception about a point of fact. For example, clients with panic disorders often have misconceived ideas about their anxiety symptoms, such as that they will go mad or that they are having a heart attack. Explanations about the nature of anxiety can be useful in these circumstances.

Analogies

Analogies can also help the client to view his thinking from a different perspective. An example of an occasion when an analogy may be useful is when a client demands that other people must treat him exactly as he want them to. The counsellor may say to the client 'Suppose that I want to be rich and I demand to have a million pounds appear in my hand, at this very moment. I must have it, I must, I must, I must.' The client can easily see that to demand this would be foolish, but the client can be shown by analogy that he is making a similarly unrealistic demand when he demands that people must treat him as he wants them to.

An example of an analogy used earlier in the book was the 'porcupine' analogy. This analogy helped the client to see the difference between opinions and facts. The client thought that he was useless because this was what someone thought of him. The counsellor challenged this conclusion. To aid in the disputation, she asked the client: 'If I thought you were a porcupine, would that mean that you were one?' Of course, the client can see that this is not true. Yet he is drawing a similar sort of conclusion when assuming that he is worthless because he has been told he is. The analogy can be helpful to illustrate the sort of thinking error the client is making.

Humour

The use of humour is recommended in the rational-emotive therapy school of CBC as a means of enabling clients to put their thinking into a more realistic perspective. This is often achieved by exaggeration of what the client is saying, to a ridiculous degree. The 'porcupine' analogy is an example of this. Humour is particularly useful in dealing with the client's self-downing statements. For example:

Client: When I went out with her I completely messed it up.
Counsellor: You mean you got her name wrong, took her to a steak-house when she's a vegetarian, and didn't say a word to her all evening?
Client: Well, it wasn't quite that bad.
Counsellor: But you would have to do that and more if you had really 'completely messed it up'.

Clearly, humour needs to be used judiciously, and always should be addressed at the client's unrealistic thinking rather than at the client as a person. Yet, bearing in mind these caveats, humour can be a useful strategy.

Modelling Other People's Adaptive Responses
Clients can usually see quite readily that other people in the same situation as themselves do not necessarily experience the same degree of emotional upset (for example, 'I know other people can brush off comments but it bothers me when people say things'). The counsellor can use this observation to show that other people do not get upset in the same way because they view the situation in a different light:

> *Counsellor*: Do you think that everyone would take Joe's criticism to heart in the way that you did?
> *Client*: I doubt it.
> *Counsellor*: If someone else were not too bothered about Joe's criticism, what would be their attitude to the comment?
> *Client*: That it didn't matter that much what Joe thought?

This method encourages the client to consider realistic alternative ways of thinking. It also enables the client to see that his reaction to the situation is not the only reaction possible and that there are other viable ways of viewing the situation.

Role Reversal
A related method is that of role reversal. This method can assist the client both to generate and practise realistic answers to negative thinking. It is particularly useful when the client has already demonstrated some skill at disputing negative thinking. In role reversal, the counsellor plays the role of client and speaks the client's negative thinking, whilst the client plays the part of the counsellor and tries to produce answers to the negative thinking.

Self-Instructional Training
The last verbal strategy we shall describe for disputing negative thinking is self-instructional training (Meichenbaum, 1985: 69–74). This involves the client learning to talk to himself in constructive ways in order to deal with extreme emotional reactions. In this approach, the client and counsellor first identify the self-defeating and stress-inducing self-statements which the client makes to himself during stressful situations. Next, they collaborate in generating alternative self-statements that encourage better problem-solving and reduce emotional disturbance. The client then memorises the coping self-statements by means of role play and imaginal practice, and then implements the statements in stressful situations.

Clearly, there is a great deal of overlap between self-instructional training (SIT) and the CBC approaches we have described. However, a difference is that SIT focuses more on the client learning specific statements to counteract negative thinking in specific high-stress situations, whereas in the CBC approaches of Ellis and Beck, the client is taught more general methods of challenging negative thinking which they can then apply in specific situations.

The more concrete SIT approach is useful for clients who have difficulty in mastering strategies for challenging negative beliefs. With these people, it can be helpful to assist the client to generate specific alternatives to negative thinking for specific problem situations. If the client is particularly unaware of his negative thinking, the counsellor can even provide plausible rational answers for the client, although obviously this is the least preferred approach since it does not encourage the client to think for himself.

In CBC, if a client faces repeated occurrences of a problematic situation, he will begin to learn specific challenges to the negative thinking which typically occurs in this situation. The client can then rehearse these rational answers before entering the situation, during the situation and afterwards, as occurs in SIT.

Imagery Methods of Modifying Maladaptive Thinking

Imagery methods can be used at three different stages of the disputing process. First, imagery can be used to help the client to generate alternatives to negative thinking. Secondly, imagery can be used to check the impact of challenges to negative thinking, and finally, the client can use imagery to rehearse alternatives to negative thinking. In the rational-emotive therapy school, such imagery methods have been developed particularly by Maultsby (1975).

Generating Alternatives to Negative Thinking
The aim of this exercise is to help the client to generate alternatives to self-defeating thinking. It can also be used to show the client the link between negative thinking and emotional upset. For this exercise, the client imagines himself in a problem situation and is encouraged to experience the same emotional disturbance that he would normally experience in the situation. The client is then asked to change the extreme negative feeling to a less disturbing, more appropriate feeling (for example, changing from depression to sadness, anger to annoyance, or anxiety to concern). The client is asked to signal to the counsellor when he has modified the feeling, and the counsellor asks the client how he managed to make the change in feelings. Typically the client says that he achieved the change in feelings by changing his

thinking about the event. Not only does this method help the client to generate alternatives to negative thinking, but it can also give the client more of a feeling of control over his emotional upsets.

Assessing Change

After helping the client to challenge negative beliefs at B, it is important for the counsellor to check with the client whether in fact there has been a resultant change in the client's emotions and behaviour at C. One way of achieving this is by means of an imagery exercise.

If a negative belief produces a generalised emotional upset (for example, the client is depressed about feeling so lethargic all the time), it may well be sufficient just to ask the client whether he feels any better as a result of disputing the negative thinking. On the other hand, if the person's upset is very situationally specific (for example, anxiety about driving), the person is less likely to experience upset about the situation in the counselling session. In this instance, it can be helpful for the client to imagine himself back in the situation to check whether his feelings associated with the situation have changed.

Imaginal Rehearsal of Alternatives to Negative Thinking

Once a particular belief or thought has been disputed in the counselling session, the client can practise using the alternative thoughts which have been generated, by imagining himself using the new thoughts in a problem situation. The client imagines himself facing the problem event and is encouraged to experience the emotional upset associated with the event. The client is then asked to practise the new realistic thinking in his imagination, and to observe the changes in his emotional reaction.

This technique can be used to help the client to become more convinced by realistic thinking, and it is particularly useful for clients who say that they cannot 'see' themselves actually facing up to a situation successfully. The exercise has one further benefit; the act of imagining a successful confrontation of the situation also increases the client's belief that he is able to control the situation and his emotions.

Distraction

Distraction is not strictly a method of changing unrealistic thinking – it is the skill of blocking out self-defeating thinking by thinking about something else. Although more enduring change can be achieved by the client challenging his unrealistic thinking, distraction has a useful place in the client's repertoire of coping skills.

There are a number of situations where a client is carrying out a task, when it may not be appropriate for him to stop the task and concentrate on challenging negative thinking. Take, for example, a self-conscious person who is having a conversation with someone and who is worrying about the other person's opinion of him. An appropriate coping strategy would be for the client to distract himself from the self-conscious thoughts by concentrating on what the other person is saying. Likewise, in some work situations it is often more functional for the client to use distraction rather than disputing, but noting the negative thinking for disputing later on.

Another occasion when distraction is useful is when the client is experiencing extreme emotional turmoil. For example, the client in a panic is usually unable to start disputing negative thinking, but can often use distraction. The challenging of negative beliefs can take place when the person has calmed down. Moreover, the realistic alternative thoughts obtained from this disputing can be used to help the client to deal with future occurrences of the problematic situation. The client can rehearse the alternative thoughts that he has generated before he enters the situation the next time.

Behavioural Methods of Modifying Maladaptive Thinking

The third main set of disputing strategies are behavioural strategies. Possibly the most powerful way for the client to modify negative thinking is to behave in a way which contradicts the negative thinking. The client sets out to test his negative thinking by carrying out behavioural tasks and evaluating the outcome. Thus the person who is afraid of going shopping is asked to enter shops. The person who sees his worth as being dependent upon doing things perfectly is asked to make some deliberate mistakes. Furthermore, the person who is afraid of rejection is asked to put himself into situations where he may be rejected. Taking this last example, the act of going into situations where he might be rejected would provide the person who fears rejection with the opportunity to learn: (1) that he can stand rejection; (2) that such rejection does not mean that he is less of a person; and (3) that rejection is not an 'awful' experience (Dryden, 1984).

Since behavioural experiments are normally carried out by the client between counselling sessions, these are discussed in more detail in Chapter 6.

Modifying Activating Events for Emotional Disturbance

So far in this chapter we have focused on how the counsellor can help the client to overcome problems by means of altering negative thinking at B in the ABC model. An alternative approach is to help the client to change the 'activating events' for his emotional disturbance.

Clients may create 'activating events' for themselves by having poor social skills or by lacking skills in personal problem-solving. Take, for example, a client who responds to a marital problem by drinking heavily, who then is fired for being drunk at work, copes badly with living on a reduced income, and batters his wife who leaves him and takes the children. Teaching this client to tackle his problems more effectively would help to reduce his emotional and behavioural disturbance by reducing the problem-situations which trigger upsets.

In a similar way, a client with poor social skills who does not know how to say 'no' to people, is likely to be taken for granted and used by other people, and this may well lead him to feel depressed and resentful. Teaching the client how to refuse requests would help to prevent the events which trigger his resentment and depression.

Poor social performance and poor problem-solving can be the result of negative thinking as well the result of poor skills, in which case they can be viewed as examples of behavioural Cs as well as As. Take, for example, a client who is depressed because he is lonely. His being alone is the activating event for his depression, but being alone might also be a behavioural consequence of his belief that he will only get rejected if he tries to make friends.

The counsellor needs to decide whether a client's poor social performance and poor problem-solving results from a skills deficit, or from negative thinking which blocks appropriate behaviour, or from a mixture of the two. Negative thinking is likely to be a more important factor if the client shows a skill in some settings but not others. For example, the person who can talk to people in small numbers, but who becomes anxious and finds it difficult to hold conversations when there is a group of people present. Similarly, a person who could solve problems effectively before he became depressed, but not after becoming depressed, is likely to be blocked more by negative thinking than by a skills deficit.

On the other hand, a skills deficit is more likely to be an important factor if a client cannot describe how to tackle a problem situation, or if the client has never shown the skill before. For example, a client who has never expressed anger to others in a direct way, may not be aware of effective and constructive ways of doing this.

Commonly, the client's poor social performance or poor problem-solving skills result from a mixture of skills deficits and self-defeating thinking. When a skills deficit is relevant to a client's problem, skills training is often carried out. Although the emphasis in CBC is on modifying beliefs, skills training is frequently useful.

Social Skills Training
Social skills training refers to procedures designed to teach clients to communicate more effectively and is mainly concerned with the verbal and non-verbal aspects of conversation and with friendship formation (see Trower et al., 1978). Examples of skills which might be taught in social skills training are: listening skills, keeping conversations going, reading social cues, and using 'body language'.

Assertiveness training is social skills training with a focus on teaching the client to express feelings and opinions in a direct but socially acceptable manner (see Chapter 9 for a more detailed description). In assertiveness training, typical areas for intervention would be: making requests, refusing requests, expressing anger, dealing with criticism, and expressing and accepting appreciation (see Lange and Jakubowski, 1976).

Social skills training incorporates the following steps: (1) identification of the skill deficit; (2) instruction about the function of the skill; (3) role play demonstration of the skill; (4) client rehearsal of the skill; (5) feedback to the client about his performance; (6) client practice of the skill in real-life situations (Trower et al., 1978). The client is assisted in the task of improving his social skills by focusing on one specific skill at a time. The client is shown how to use the skill, he then practises the skill himself in a role-play situation, and is then given feedback about his performance. The client practises the skill again, this time incorporating the feedback. Finally, the client carries out homework tasks which help him to put the skills he has learned into practice.

Problem-Solving Training
Clients with poor problem-solving skills can be taught a series of steps to help them think through problems and solutions and to help them cope with problems in a more constructive way. The steps of problem-solving are as follows (see Spivack et al., 1976): (a) define the problem; (b) generate possible solutions to the problem; (c) evaluate the solutions and select the optimum solution; (d) plan how to implement the preferred solution.

These steps can be written out for the client on a sheet of paper, leaving spaces beneath each step for the client's responses. The counsellor first works through one of the client's problems with the client in the counselling session, and then asks the client to select another problem and to complete the problem-solving sheet as a homework task.

Often the client finds difficulty in specifying the exact nature of the problem, especially when the problem involves other people who may take a different view of the situation. Another difficulty is that clients find it hard to generate alternative solutions, for negative thinking about how the problem can be tackled will often lead the client to discard potential solutions out of hand. It is necessary therefore to encourage clients to write down all possible solutions, even if they seem at first to be bad ones. Help may be necessary to enable the client to evaluate the consequences of the various solutions and select the best one. It may also be necessary to dispute cognitive blocks to the client carrying out a potential solution.

It is important to note that there may not be any satisfactory solution to the problem, although the chosen option may be the best available option. At the least, problem-solving can help the client to clarify issues, but there is often a way of tackling a problem which is a step better than the way the client is currently tackling it. One final point is that the most workable solution for the client may not be the solution which the counsellor herself would choose in the situation, and the inexperienced counsellor should be wary of pushing the client too hard towards a solution which the client does not favour.

Creating Emotional and Behavioural Change
When assessing the effectiveness of counselling, the counsellor will want to see emotional and behavioural change before she will be convinced that changes have occurred in the client's thinking.

After the counsellor and client have challenged a dysfunctional belief, the client is likely to believe at least to some extent in a more realistic way of viewing the situation. However, this belief in realistic alternatives to the dysfunctional beliefs may be weak, and when confronted with the problem situation again, the client may well revert to his unrealistic thinking. In order to sustain enduring changes in his emotional life and behaviour, the client must consolidate his realistic beliefs and move from being weakly convinced by more functional beliefs to being more strongly convinced by them.

We have dealt elsewhere with the key strategies for helping the client strengthen his conviction in alternative, functional beliefs. In Chapter 4, we described the use and development of emotional insight (as opposed to intellectual insight) to change core beliefs, including a procedure for vividly re-experiencing an emotional episode, and a mood induction procedure for experiencing a change in feelings following systematic alternative thinking. In the next chapter we describe homework procedures for achieving conviction by repetition, in which the client is shown how to undertake persistent practice in tasks which give the opportunity to rehearse thoughts which contradict negative beliefs.

6 Homework Tasks

General Strategies in Setting Homework Tasks

The main part of the therapeutic work in CBC has to be carried out by the client between counselling sessions. The counsellor encourages the client to put into practice and consolidate what has been discussed in the counselling session, by helping the client to decide suitable tasks to be completed before the next session. Discussion of homework tasks should therefore be given due emphasis in the counselling sessions, and fifteen to twenty minutes may be needed for setting the homework task or assignment.

The task needs to be discussed and agreed between the client and counsellor, for if the client helps to decide the task, the task is more likely to be relevant to his problems and the client is more likely to be committed to carrying it out. Moreover, by taking part in the decision-making process, the client is learning how to set tasks for himself and how to develop his own therapeutic programme.

In order to maximise the chances that the client will actually carry out the task, the homework needs to be very specific. It should include exactly what the client has to do, when and under what conditions. Another important point is that tasks which involve challenging a particular belief need to be carried out several times in the week – not just once. It can be helpful to specify a minimum number of times for the task to be completed, perhaps three or five times depending on the task.

Once a task has been agreed, it is important to ask the client what he thinks the aim of the task is. The counsellor can think she has explained things clearly to the client, yet a simple check often reveals misunderstandings.

Next, the counsellor checks the client's commitment to the task by asking whether the client thinks that he will carry out the task and whether he can foresee any particular difficulties in doing so. Such difficulties may be practical (for example, there is nowhere quiet to do reading), or they may be cognitive (for example, 'it sounds alright, but I just can't see myself doing it'). Once the nature of the block has been identified, the counsellor can help the client to problem-solve practical problems and dispute cognitive blocks. It can also be helpful for the client to rehearse the task in imagination or by means of role-play (see Chapter 5).

One further strategy is to set up the homework task as a no-lose situation. The counsellor impresses upon the client that if he succeeds on the task that is good, but that if the client fails on the task, useful information can still be gained about the negative thinking that blocks the client, and an opportunity is provided for him to learn that the consequences of failure are never catastrophic.

During the early stages of counselling, homework tasks are directed towards making the client more aware of his thinking and emotions, and teaching him about CBC. As far as learning about CBC is concerned, the client may be asked to read material about this form of counselling. The reading material may consist of the counsellor's own handouts on CBC or books such as those by Ellis and Harper (1975), Emery (1982), Hauck (1974), Burns (1980), Lembo (1977) or Blackburn (1987).

Thought Recording

Helping the client to become more aware of his thinking and emotions may be achieved by getting the client to keep a diary or record of emotional upsets and problem situations. What exactly is recorded will depend upon the nature of the person's problem, but a record might, for example, be kept of panic attacks, unassertive behaviour, or depressed mood. The ABC form described in Chapter 3 (Figure 1) can be used as a thought record, to teach the client to recognise negative thinking and its effects on feelings. For the initial task of teaching the client the connections between his thoughts and emotions, only part of the form is used (columns 1, 2 and 4), as shown in Figure 2.

The client completes the record whenever he feels upset in any way. First, he records in column four how he feels (emotional C) and any self-defeating behaviour (behavioural C). After recording these, the client records in column one the situation (A) which occurred when he started to experience the negative emotions. This might have been a clear-cut event such as walking into a room full of people, or it might have been that the client was simply sitting and thinking. Finally, the client records in column two what was running through his mind just before he started to feel bad. This may be either a thought or an image.

There is no set number of times that the client has to fill in the form – the client should simply record whenever he feels disturbed in any way. Ideally the client should complete the form as soon as the emotional upset has occurred, but this is often not practicable (for example, in some work situations). However, the record needs to be made as soon as possible in order for the client to recall his thoughts

| Activating event | Beliefs (about A) | | Consequences (of B) | |
Describe actual or anticipated event 1	List dysfunctional thoughts/images 2	List functional alternative thoughts/images 3	List dysfunctional emotions/behaviours 4	List functional emotions/behaviours 5
Meeting ex-girlfriend in the street	I'll never find another girlfriend like her.	I do miss her badly, but there is no reason why I won't meet someone else. I did have a lot of rows with Susan, so I might even find someone I get on with better.	Depressed	Sad
	I'll never be happy without her.	I was happy before I met her so I should be able to get back to being happy when I've got over Susan.	Depressed	Sad

Figure 2 A completed ABC form

clearly. Some clients prefer to record negative thoughts using a notebook rather than a form because a notebook can easily be carried in a pocket and is less conspicuous.

When explaining thought recording to the client, it is helpful for the counsellor to work through an example with the client. The counsellor can use an example of an incident drawn from the client's own experience – preferably an example from the recent past so that the client can remember it clearly.

Common Problems with Thought Recording

Sometimes a client says that his emotional upsets come 'out of the blue', and that he is not thinking of anything when he starts to feel bad. This is usually just a case of the client not being aware of negative thinking, and with practice the client learns to identify the negative thinking. Another mistake clients make is to write down thoughts which do not explain the emotional upset. For example, the client may report feeling very guilty yet record thoughts such as: 'Well, it can't be helped.' Clearly if this were all that the client was thinking, he would not have felt guilty in the way he did. This can be pointed out to the client by asking a question such as, 'If this were all you were thinking, do you think you would feel so guilty?' Another problem can be that the clients write down a lot of extraneous thoughts in addition to upsetting thoughts and again it is necessary to teach the client to record only the relevant emotive thoughts.

Recording Challenges to Negative Thinking

After one or two weeks of recording negative thoughts, the client is usually ready to start completing the whole of the form shown in Figure 2. This requires the client not only to record negative thinking, but also to challenge the negative thinking and record the outcome. Once the client has recorded his negative thoughts and feelings, he then enters into column 3, realistic alternatives to the negative thinking described in column 2. After writing down these challenges to the negative thinking, the client records in column 5 how he feels as a result of the functional alternative thoughts, and how he would respond to the situation when he is thinking in this more functional way. An illustration of a completed record form is shown in Figure 2. Beck et al. (1979), Emery (1985) and Ellis and Harper (1975) all suggest variations of this type of form.

Reviewing the Completion of ABC Forms

It is common for clients to experience difficulty in generating realistic challenges to negative thinking, although clients can vary quite considerably in how quickly they learn this skill. It is usually necessary to work through a number of examples with the client before he is able to challenge negative thinking independently. As described above, the counsellor will sometimes find that the client records thoughts which do not match the reported emotion. Similarly, clients sometimes record realistic challenges which sound plausible but which do not directly answer the negative thoughts. For example:

Emotion	*Negative thinking*	*Rational answer*
Depression	I'm being punished for my wrong-doings	This won't last forever

Here the counsellor needs to point this out to the client and help him to develop a rational response which directly answers his negative thought.

When the counsellor reviews the disputing record, she needs to check whether the client is feeling any better after the challenging of particular negative thoughts. If the client feels even a little better, the counsellor should emphasise this improvement. Becoming convinced about realistic alternatives to negative thinking is a gradual process, and therefore the client needs to expect and be encouraged by small changes.

A useful way to emphasise the gradual nature of changes in negative thinking is to ask the client to rate on a 0–100 per cent scale how much he believes in each functional thought. A score of 0 per cent would mean that the client had no belief in a thought, and a score of 100 per cent would mean that the client had total conviction in the thought. In a similar way, the client can rate the strength of his negative emotions on each occasion. The percentage ratings of belief in thoughts and strength of emotions are useful in that the client can see that his negative emotions gradually reduce as the strength of his conviction about the functional beliefs builds up. This assists the client in moving away from seeing progress in 'either-or' terms (either he has made considerable progress, or he has not made any progress at all).

It will not be possible in a single session for the counsellor to review in detail all the emotional disturbances the client may record on the disputing form, so it will be necessary to ask the client to choose one or two incidents which he would like to discuss. It is far more effective in a session to dispute one or two beliefs thoroughly than to discuss a number of beliefs without achieving any cognitive change.

Checklist to Aid the Challenging of Negative Thoughts
A short checklist of questions can be helpful as an aid to challenging negative thinking which can be used by the client in combination with

the ABC form. The questions are of the sort which the counsellor would ask the client during disputing. Below is an example of such a checklist for an anxious patient.

1 What exactly is it that I am worried about?
2 Is it really likely to happen? Is it true? What is the evidence?
3 Supposing the worst does happen – would it be the end of the world? What is the evidence that it would be terrible?

The following example, showing answers to the questions, will illustrate the use of the checklist:

Q1: 'If they see I'm anxious, they'll think I'm really stupid.'
Q2: 'They may well not notice, and if they do there's no reason why they should think I'm stupid because of it. It may not bother them at all.'
Q3: 'Just because they think I'm stupid does not mean I am. You're not stupid just because you're anxious. Anyway, nothing disastrous would happen even if they did think I was stupid.'

The client can carry a copy of the checklist around with him to aid disputing whenever a worry or problem situation occurs. The checklist is most helpful if the client writes out the answers to the questions onto the ABC form. Writing out the answers to negative thinking helps to clarify the issues for the client. Moreover, the client has a permanent record of the challenges to negative thinking which he can read in order to memorise them. The client can then rehearse these challenges in order to help him cope with future situations. With repeated use of the checklist and thought record form, the client gradually starts to challenge his negative thinking automatically, as it occurs.

Behavioural Tasks

Behavioural tasks are tasks that require the client to carry out some activity that is feared or avoided or to desist from carrying out some habitual behaviour that is unhelpful. The aim of behavioural tasks is twofold. First, there is evidence that behaving as if you hold a certain point of view increases your belief in that point of view (Festinger, 1957). Therefore, one way for a client to increase his conviction in realistic thinking is to engage in behaviours that contradict the negative thoughts.

A second and related aim of behavioural tasks is to help the client to gather evidence relating to his negative beliefs. This evidence can be used in the client's disputing of negative thinking. Take, for example, a client who was afraid to say 'no' to his demanding father. His father would ask his son to do a lot of things for him which he could quite easily manage himself. The client believed that if he said 'no', his father would get very angry and would never speak to him again. By refusing to do things for his father, the client learned that although his father was annoyed, he had over-estimated the strength of his father's negative reaction. Moreover, he learned that he could refuse some of his father's requests despite receiving a negative reaction, and that having his father be annoyed with him was not so awful.

Some further examples of behavioural tasks are given below.

Problem	Behavioural task
Fear of rejection	Doing something which opens the person to the possibility of being rejected (e.g. asking a favour, asking for a date, making a request).
Perfectionism	Deliberately making a mistake (in something that does not matter too much) or letting something go which has not been completed quite correctly (e.g. a letter with mistakes).
Fear of panicking	Gradually going into situations where panics may occur (e.g. shops).
Procrastination	Carrying out whichever activities are being put off (e.g. making a career decision).

Behavioural tasks follow on from disputing in the counselling session. Once a particular belief has been challenged, the counsellor and client attempt to construct a behavioural experiment which tests the belief, and which gives the client practice in behaving in a more adaptive way. These tasks commonly consist of behaving in the opposite way to the behavioural C.

With some beliefs where there is a clearly avoided behaviour, such as when a person avoids social situations because he 'couldn't bear' people seeing that he was anxious, it is relatively easy to design a behavioural task. The task would be to carry out the avoided activity in order to disprove the unrealistic thinking (for example, that it would be unbearable if people saw that he was anxious).

On the other hand, with some beliefs it is difficult to imagine a suitable behavioural task. For example, the depressed client who believes that he is an awful person for getting so depressed and letting down his family. In this case, the person could not carry out an empirical test of whether he is an awful person. In cases such as this, when suitable tasks are not apparent, the emphasis will necessarily revolve around verbal challenging of the self-defeating thinking, as described in the last section.

A client can make a behavioural task more effective and easier to carry out, by combining the behavioural challenging of the negative thoughts with verbal challenging of the negative thoughts. Before he carries out the task, the client needs to rehearse the challenges to the negative thinking which have been worked out in the counselling session, and add any further challenges of his own. One way for the client to do this is to go through the situation in his mind's eye – imagining himself disputing the self-defeating thinking and carrying out the task successfully. The client then needs to continue the verbal challenging of the self-defeating thoughts when he is actually carrying out the task.

Risk-Taking and Shame-Attacking Exercises
The two main types of behavioural tasks used in the rational-emotive school of CBC are risk-taking exercises and shame-attacking exercises (this section owes much to Wessler and Wessler, 1980).

Risk-taking exercises are tasks which involve the client taking some sort of risk – usually a social risk such as a risk of rejection or failure. The client carries out a task which may produce an undesired outcome which the client views as dangerous, for example, a perfectionist not doing something properly. The aim of the exercise is for the client to re-evaluate the negative outcome as neither terrible nor dangerous, and to teach the client that he does not need to denigrate himself for failing or being rejected. Clearly, the counsellor should not advise the client to carry out exercises which might have serious consequences for the client, consequences which might, for example, jeopardise the person's job or cause unreasonable offence. Seemingly mild risk-taking exercises could feasibly have serious consequences; for example, being assertive with a spouse might be the 'last straw' in the relationship, and so the counsellor needs to discuss and assess the potential dangers with the client.

How difficult an exercise is chosen is determined as a result of negotiation with the client. The degree of risk involved in a task is an individual matter, and what is considered risky for one person may not be for another. Commonly the counsellor's suggestion is considered by the client to be too hard. The client may then suggest a less risky alternative. If the client agrees too readily, the task is probably too easy and a task of medium difficulty should be negotiated.

When a client is unable to carry out an exercise because he thinks it is too difficult, one method of reducing the client's anxiety is for him to rehearse carrying out the task in imagination or by means of role-play. Another approach is for the counsellor to carry out the task *in vivo* with the client, with the counsellor modelling the task first. Shame-attacking exercises are based upon the idea that a person's self-worth does not depend on his behaviour. Shame occurs when a person devalues himself for behaving in a way which attracts disapproval or ridicule. Thus shame-attacking exercises involve the client carrying out some kind of act which is designed deliberately to attract disapproval or ridicule from others, thereby giving the client an opportunity to learn that disapproval and ridicule is not devastating, nor need the client denigrate himself because of it. Examples of shame-attacking exercises would be to shout something out in a busy street or to walk around wearing odd clothing.

Shame-attacking exercises are similar to risk-taking exercises except that the task carried out in shame-attacking exercises invites rejection or disapproval, and the emphasis is on tackling the client's self-devaluation.

The strategies for negotiating shame-attacking exercises are very similar to those used with risk-taking exercises; and as with risk-taking exercises, the task has to be tailored to that individual client – what may be shameful for one person may not be shameful for another.

When using shame-attacking exercises with clients one caution is in order. Clients should be discouraged from acting in a way that may have serious negative consequences for themselves (e.g. acting stupidly at work and thereby getting fired or breaking the law and getting themselves arrested) or in a way that may unduly alarm others.

Reviewing Homework

Needless to say, it is important for the counsellor to review the client's homework when he next sees the client. Completion of homework tasks is central to the success of CBC and should therefore be given adequate attention in the counselling sessions. It would also be very discouraging for the client to have put a lot of effort into the homework, only to find that the counsellor pays little attention to it.

Even when the client has completed the homework, it is useful to check carefully the client's perception of how well the homework went, and the client's evaluation of his performance. If the client has a bias towards negative thinking, he is likely to appraise the homework in a negative light. He may think that the homework went disastrously, and that this is further proof that he is a failure. Questioning about what actually happened may reveal that the client completed the task quite adequately but failed to live up to his unrealistically high expectations. Take, for example, the client whose homework was to have a conversation with a colleague at work. He did have the conversation but thought he had messed it up because there was an awkward silence in the middle. Black-or-white thinking like this is common – if the personal performance or the situation is not completely right, then it is viewed as completely wrong.

Even in cases where the client has failed on the task, this still does not justify negative self-evaluations such as that the client is a failure, and useful work can be carried out in tackling these over-generalised and self-deprecatory thoughts.

Blocks to the Completion of Homework Tasks

If the client has not completed the task, it will be necessary to uncover the reasons why. One of the strengths of CBC is that it provides a method for looking at why therapeutic tasks are not carried out. First, however, the counsellor needs to check that the client has understood the task and has understood how executing it would help him to achieve his goals (for example, to overcome his fear of social situations). The counsellor will have already worked through this process in the previous session when the homework task was set, but however carefully this preparation was carried out, some clients will have lost sight of the purpose of the task and how it might help them.

Next, the counsellor looks for negative thinking which may have blocked the client from carrying out the task. Generally this negative thinking is one of two types:

'What is the point? . . .'
'It's too difficult . . . (and it shouldn't be).'

'What is the point?' is a form of helplessness or hopelessness where the client thinks that the task is not worth trying. He may see himself as incapable of effecting any change in his life, and think that he has tried everything, and that nothing he can do will help the situation. Alternatively, he may not believe that doing the task could make any significant difference to his problem.

When the client is negative about the value of the task, the counsellor is unlikely to be able to persuade the client to be enthusiastic about it, but he is aiming to convince the client that he could physically carry out the task, that the task *might* help, and that it is worth a try.

This change of attitude is achieved by reviewing the evidence for and against the beliefs that the task is pointless. What are the potential advantages of trying the task? What are the consequences of not trying the task (for example, getting more depressed)? It is helpful to remind the client of the ancient Chinese proverb that even the longest journey begins with the first step. The counsellor encourages the client that he *can* gradually overcome his problems if only he would make the first steps.

The 'It's too difficult' block occurs when the client sees the task as a bigger obstacle than it is, or when there is an unwillingness to tolerate the hard work needed to reduce the problem. Ellis (1979) has suggested that the major reason why people fail to change is because of a philosophy of 'low frustration tolerance'. This is a philosophy that 'Life must be comfortable and easy, and go the way I want it to'. Furthermore, if life is not comfortable and easy: 'That is awful' and 'I can't stand it.' Moreover, some clients want an instant cure and are intolerant of the discomfort of slow progress.

Low frustration tolerance can be a block to progress with many emotional and behavioural problems: for example, the anxious person who avoids a task of talking to people for fear of becoming uncomfortably anxious. Alternatively, the inactive, depressed person who avoids the discomfort involved in a task of carrying out more activities, or finally, the person who fails to give up smoking because he cannot tolerate the agitation he experiences.

A central feature of low frustration tolerance as we have shown is that the client is saying that he cannot stand that which he does not like. As with other maladaptive beliefs, this belief can be challenged by asking the client for the evidence that he cannot stand the discomfort (rather than the fact that he just dislikes the discomfort). Clearly, carrying out homework tasks can be difficult and unpleasant for a client. However, sometimes the client needs to be faced with the fact that he has a choice between continuing the more comfortable path of doing nothing about his problem, or tolerating further discomfort with the prospect of longer-term gains. Stressing the long-term disadvantages of failing to tackle the problem may also be helpful, for it is often these negative factors that have led the client to seek counselling.

Finally, an encouraging point to note is that low frustration tolerance often diminishes once the client has started to experience positive benefits from the counselling, when he realises that the effort he is making is having a worthwhile result.

In this chapter, we have reviewed strategies for designing, negotiating and reviewing homework tasks. In the remaining chapters we look at specific problem areas, and highlight common sorts of unrealistic thinking, together with a description of methods particularly useful with each type of problem.

PART III   COMMON EMOTIONAL PROBLEMS

In the remaining chapters, we move from describing general CBC skills to describing the application of CBC to specific emotional problems. Chapter 7 focuses on anxiety, Chapter 8 on depression, and in Chapter 9 we turn to shame, guilt and anger. Chapter 9 also includes a section on assertiveness training.

These chapters provide a description of the common features of each emotional problem, and the aims of CBC in each case. Guidance is then given about identifying the particular belief systems underlying each emotion, together with advice about a range of useful cognitive-behavioural methods. Finally, a description is given of some of the pitfalls encountered when carrying out CBC with these types of problems.

7 Anxiety

Anxiety occurs when a person thinks there is some kind of threat. This may take the form of a physical danger such as a fear of having a heart-attack, or a social danger such as a fear of being rejected. Anxious thinking usually concerns future events – often 'what if . . .' thinking.

Lazarus (1966) has identified two stages of appraisal when a person becomes anxious. First, the person judges whether the situation he is confronting is a threat. To do this he estimates the probability of the harmful outcome occurring, and assesses the degree of potential harm. At the second stage, the person estimates his ability to cope and deal with the threat. The degree of anxiety experienced is therefore determined by both how threatening the situation seems to be and by the person's confidence in his ability to cope with the situation. When a person has an anxiety disorder, he functions like an over-sensitive alarm system (Beck, 1985) and tends to overestimate danger and underestimate coping resources.

A whole range of sensations may be experienced by someone who is anxious. Common physiological symptoms include heart-racing, shortness of breath, rapid breathing, shaking, feeling weak, nausea, faintness, muscle-tension and sweating. There are also behavioural symptoms such as fidgeting and pacing up and down. With anxiety, there is a tendency for the person to withdraw from or avoid situations that are seen as threatening. This brings relief in the short-term, but has destructive effects in the long-term as more and more situations are avoided. Examples of avoidance are when a person procrastinates over decisions, avoids social situations, or tries to drown feelings by means of alcohol or drug abuse.

Alternatively, in the case of obsessive-compulsive disorders (which often require more intensive therapy and are thus outside the scope of this book), there may be attempts to reduce anxiety by carrying out compulsive behaviours such as checking things or completing rituals (for example, doing things a certain number of times or in a certain way). Carrying out these compulsive behaviours seems to reduce the anxiety of someone with this problem in the short term, because the client believes that something disastrous will happen if he does not carry out the compulsive behaviour.

Finally, there is a common tendency for an anxious person to seek reassurance from other people. Again, this may reduce anxiety in the short-term, but the repeated seeking of reassurance undermines the person's confidence to deal with the problem himself.

Thinking Errors

In all anxiety problems, there is a tendency for the person to overestimate the probability of bad things occurring and to catastrophise about the consequences of this predicted bad event. There is therefore usually a mistaken inference (overestimating the probability of the unpleasant event happening) and a mistaken evaluation (evaluating the outcome of the unpleasant event to be disastrous).

An anxious person also shows what Beck (1985) has termed 'selective abstraction': the tendency to be hypersensitive to the threatening aspects of situations and ignore the positive or benign aspects of situations.

Dichotomous thinking is another form of thinking error shown by anxious people (Beck, 1985). Unless a situation is unmistakably safe, it is likely to be perceived as unsafe. Ambiguous situations are viewed as threatening (for example, an ambiguous comment or expression on someone's face). This sort of thinking is common in performance anxiety where a person who makes a small mistake (for example, has hesitant speech as a result of anxiety) may view himself as completely messing up the whole interaction with the other person.

Types of Anxiety Problem

Anxiety problems tend to fall into patterns of disorder, and each disorder is characterised by certain types of anxious thinking. The specific sub-type of anxiety makes little difference to treatment from a CBC point of view, for the same principles and general approach apply in each case. However, the description of the sorts of fears which are prevalent in each sub-type will help the counsellor to know what sorts of anxious thinking to look out for. The descriptions given below are drawn from the revised third edition of the *Diagnostic and Statistical Manual of Mental Disorders* (APA, 1987).

Panic Disorder

In panic disorder, the client experiences recurrent panics, that is, discrete periods of intense fear. During a panic, the person feels overwhelmed by anxiety and it is often the loss of control which is a central feature of the person's fear. Associated with this loss of control, there are often fears of fainting, of being sick, or of acting in some bizarre way. In addition, there may be fears that passers-by might notice the client's anxiety and disapprove of or ridicule the client. The client may even think he will go mad or die. Fears of heart-attacks are common, and occasionally people interpret their shortness of breath as indicative that they will stop breathing and die. Clearly, it is necessary to get to the bottom of the client's fears about what will happen to him when he has a panic. If the client actually thinks he is going to die when he has a panic, no wonder he feels anxious! The client's fear about the possibility of having a panic may even trigger the panic; the worries about panicking make the client anxious, and these internal sensations are then interpreted by the client as evidence that he is starting to lose control. The thought that he is losing control creates more anxiety, and a vicious circle is set up whereby the client becomes more and more anxious.

One further feature worth noting about panic attacks is that some clients perpetuate the panic by over-breathing. When anxious, some clients take rapid shallow breaths, or large gulps of air, and the physiological effects of this are light-headedness, dizziness and tingling feelings which are similar to the anxiety symptoms of panic. These sensations are usually interpreted by the client as part of the panic, and are evaluated in a catastrophic fashion, which in turn leads to further over-breathing. Hence a vicious circle of anxious thinking and over-breathing is created.

Agoraphobia
In agoraphobia, there is a central fear of being trapped in places from which it is difficult to leave without attracting attention. The person is afraid of developing incapacitating or potentially embarrassing symptoms such as feeling dizzy, fainting, having a heart-attack or vomiting.

When a person avoids situations because of a fear such as that of vomiting in public, the person may have the fear without actually having panic attacks. However, panic attacks and agoraphobia very commonly go together, and in both sorts of problem there is a strong fear of losing control.

As a result of his fears, the person with agoraphobia avoids difficult situations, or endures them whilst experiencing intense anxiety. Common situations that are avoided are being in crowds, buses, shops, supermarkets, hairdressers, and trains. In severe cases, the person may be virtually housebound, not daring to go anywhere alone. Typically the person feels safer when going out accompanied by another person, who would be able to help the person if necessary. There is therefore often dependence on a spouse to help the client with the problem.

Simple Phobias
Simple phobias are irrational fears of common objects or situations such as spiders, dogs, heights, enclosed spaces, blood and injections. There is an intense desire to avoid the feared situation, and although the phobic situation may be quite specific, the fear may have a very restrictive effect on the person's life. For example, the client with a phobia of dogs may be afraid to walk along the street in case he meets a dog, or one with a phobia of thunder may feel agitated whenever it is cloudy or humid as then there is a possibility of thunder.

The person with a phobia sees the feared situation as dangerous, but the belief about how dangerous the situation is will usually vary according to the client's proximity to the situation. When calm, a person with a phobia of lifts may rate the probability of getting trapped in a lift to be remote. However, when confronted with the actual situation he will become certain that he will get trapped.

Social Phobia
Whereas the person with agoraphobia is more concerned with the consequences of having an anxiety attack when alone or when trapped in a situation, the person with social phobia is anxious about any situation in which he may be observed or scrutinised by others. He is fearful of being evaluated negatively by others, for example, being rejected or thought of as inadequate or inferior. He is therefore afraid of acting in some way which would result in disapproval or rejection, and which would lead him to feel humiliated or embarrassed.

Common problem situations include being introduced to people, meeting people in authority, using the telephone, being watched doing something, eating or writing in front of people, and public speaking (Amies et al., 1983). Difficulties in dealing with these kinds of situations often lead to avoidance of the situations, and as in agoraphobia, there is a downward spiral effect with the person avoiding more and more, as he feels less and less confident. Such clients often seek counselling help because they have become lonely as a result of their avoidance of social situations, and they may also feel quite depressed. Another common reason for seeking help is when the client is having difficulties with work relationships.

The person with social phobia is typically concerned about the disruptive effect of his anxiety on his social performance. Whereas the fears of the person with agoraphobia about the consequences of his anxiety are often unrealistic (for example, having a heart attack), the fears of the person with social anxiety may often actually materialise (for example, not being able to think what to say, having unclear speech) (Beck, 1985). However, the client with social anxiety is also likely to catastrophise about the outcome of this impaired social performance (for example, he may think that people will always be bored by him and that he will never be able to make any friends).

Socially anxious clients are very sensitive to other people's reactions to them, and they often anticipate critical evaluation from others. For example, one client was seen sunbathing by his neighbour, and he immediately thought that the neighbours would think how ugly he was.

Socially anxious people also tend to hold unrealistically high expectations for their own performance. They are therefore very sensitive to failure in social situations and tend to devalue themselves for failing to achieve their own expectations. For example, one man thought he was a failure because he did not join in conversations and games of cards with his work colleagues at break-times.

Self-Fulfilling Prophecy. The fear of negative evaluation of the person with social phobia often becomes a self-fulfilling prophecy (Trower and Turland, 1984). This occurs in two ways. First, the client's beliefs lead him to behave in a way which elicits a negative reaction from others. Take, for example, Bill, an anxious client who believes that other people will find him boring. When in a conversation with someone, Bill's anxiety leads him to avoid other people's eye gaze and to say very little. This behaviour produces a negative reaction in others who think that Bill is not very friendly. This negative reaction then seems to Bill to be confirmatory evidence for his initial prediction that he is boring.

The second way in which the self-fulfilling prophecy operates is by the process of selective perception. Bill, who thinks he is boring, tends to notice and recall the negative aspects of his interactions and ignore the positive. So he might notice the awkward pause in the middle of his conversation, but fail to notice that the other person seemed to have enjoyed the conversation. Thus, the person with social phobia is confirming his negative beliefs by selecting out evidence in agreement with these beliefs.

Social Anxiety and Social Skills. As will be apparent from the discussion so far, there is a close link between social anxiety and social skills. Since anxiety disrupts social performance, the socially anxious person can appear socially unskilled. Moreover, if the anxiety is prolonged the client may lose his ability to use his skills, even though he may be able to describe the skilled way to behave in social situations. If prolonged social anxiety occurs at a critical period (for example, during adolescence), it may prevent the learning of skills (for example, courtship).

The picture of social skills and anxiety is further complicated by the fact that socially unskilled people are likely to fail in social situations and that this failure is likely to provoke anxiety. Therefore, clients appearing with social anxiety may or may not be socially unskilled, and it will be necessary to assess whether skills training is necessary. This assessment can be made from the client's description of his interactions, and from observation of his behaviour in the interview (at first meeting, one prospective candidate for a social skills training group walked into the counsellor's office, remarked how smoky it was and opened the window!).

Generalised Anxiety Disorder
In the case of generalised anxiety disorder, the client experiences persistent and generalised anxiety and worry about his life circumstances. The anxiety is not associated with specific situations as with phobic problems, but arises from the person's worries about life problems. In the case of phobias, the client may feel calm when in a 'safe' situation, whereas with generalised anxiety disorder the client is unable to relax. The most common features of generalised anxiety disorder are: inability to relax, tension, difficulty concentrating, feeling frightened and on edge, feeling weak and unsteady, and fear of losing control and being rejected (Beck, 1985).

Often a person's anxiety problem will begin when he worries about things such as personal relationships, work or financial problems, or difficulties with family or neighbours. However, once the anxiety problem is established, the person is often more concerned with the consequences of the anxiety; he worries about his health, that other people will notice his anxiety, he worries about his difficulty in thinking clearly, and his general inability to cope.

As with other anxiety problems, loss of confidence is a major feature of the generalised anxiety problem. The difficulty is not just that the person tends to overestimate the danger of his life situation, the person also underestimates his ability to cope with problems. The loss of confidence may follow one or two major stressful events, or may result in a general increase in demands on the person beyond his ability to cope (for example, getting increased responsibility at work at the same time as having a child). Alternatively, there may be a reduction in the amount of social support the person receives (anxiety difficulties often begin after a person moves to a place where they do not have friends). Finally, a loss of confidence often occurs after the person's physical resources have been reduced, by illness, for example.

Aims of CBC for Anxiety
In CBC, the aim is for the anxious client to make a more realistic estimation of the probability of the feared event occurring, and to

make a more realistic evaluation of the consequences of the event should it happen. Some clients initially worry that if they are less anxious about a problem situation, this will take away their motivation to change the problem. However, quite the opposite is true; when not paralysed by anxiety, the client is much more likely to view the problem as something which is within his power to tackle. The client is therefore much more likely to confront the threat and deal successfully with it, than avoid or withdraw from it as usually occurs with anxiety.

Specific Strategies for Working with Anxious Clients

Three Components of Anxiety
Anxiety can be divided into three inter-related components or systems: the cognitive, behavioural and somatic. The cognitive component refers to the client's anxious thinking and imagery. The behavioural component refers to the client's avoidance of difficult situations or avoidance of facing up to problems, and the somatic component concerns the client's physical symptoms such as tension or dizziness.

This categorisation of anxiety is useful from a practical point of view because the counsellor can utilise strategies to tackle each aspect of anxiety. We will now take each component of anxiety and describe strategies that are useful in each case.

Cognitive Aspects of Anxiety
Fear of Fear. A key part of CBC for clients with anxiety problems is to tackle the client's self-defeating beliefs about his anxiety. The client is usually frightened by his symptoms and, as described above, may have all sorts of anxious beliefs about his anxiety (for example, thinking he will have a heart-attack or fearing ridicule because of his anxiety). This fear of fear is often a major factor in perpetuating anxiety problems and needs to be tackled near the beginning of the counselling.

One way to identify a client's fears about his anxiety is to get him to describe an anxiety-provoking situation, and then to ask him what he thinks would happen if he became extremely anxious. If necessary, the counsellor can use probes such as, 'Do you think you would come to any physical harm?' or 'Would it bother you a great deal if other people saw you were anxious?' The sorts of fears that clients have about their anxiety are illustrated above in the descriptions of the various types of anxiety problem.

In some instances, the counsellor may be able to help simply by giving the client information about anxiety which counteracts misconceptions (that the client, for example, will not go 'mad' as a result of a panic attack). In other cases, she will help the client to weigh up the evidence for and against his self-defeating inferences and evaluations. For example, with the client who is afraid that he would be sick in public, the counsellor would help the client to weigh up the evidence that this would happen (has it happened before?). Note that very often clients' fears have some factual basis, and so it is à mistake for the counsellor to jump in with reassurance that the feared outcome will not occur. She needs to ask the client, 'What makes you think that your fear will come true?'

After helping the client to question the inference that he will be sick in public, the counsellor would help the client to evaluate how negative the consequences would be if he were sick. Using a questioning technique, the counsellor would help the client to see that although it might be very unpleasant to be sick, it would not be awful – a lot worse could have happened, and long-term or major negative consequences would be unlikely. The counsellor would also help the client to deal with his embarrassment by helping him see that being sick could not mean he was an awful person (see section on embarrassment in Chapter 9).

Clients usually find it easier to challenge unrealistic inferences about the likelihood of a feared event than to challenge the unrealistic evaluations that they make about the consequences of the event were it to occur. However, the counsellor needs to persevere in tackling the clients' overly negative evaluations about feared events because this is the more powerful solution to the client's problems (since any bad event *may* happen).

Situationally Specific Fear. Since a client's anxiety may be specific to particular problem situations, the client may describe his fears in the counselling session but not actually feel anxious in the interview. This is sometimes a problem if the client is not able to identify the anxious thoughts occurring when he is anxious. In such cases, it can be helpful for the counsellor to get the client to imagine himself in the feared situation. In order to do this, the counsellor encourages the client to recall in detail a recent instance when he became anxious. She asks the client to recall the incident with his eyes closed and to signal by lifting a finger whenever he starts to feel anxious. At this point, the counsellor asks the client to try to identify what was running through his mind just as he was starting to feel anxious. This procedure often produces fresh material for the counsellor to work on.

A common problem in CBC with anxious clients occurs during the disputing of anxious thinking. The anxious client may readily see the irrationality of his anxious thinking when he is removed from the feared situation, but rapidly loses this realistic perspective when faced with the real situation. It is helpful if the counsellor anticipates this obstacle and makes suggestions about how the problem can be overcome.

One solution is for the client to memorise challenges to his fears in the situation, for this will help the client to access these realistic thoughts more easily when in the real situation. Alternatively, the client may write down the realistic alternative thoughts on a small card, and carry this around with him to read just before he enters the problematic situation, or even during it. When panicky, the client may find it too difficult to generate answers to anxious thinking on the spot. He is likely to find it much easier to read through the realistic thoughts. This strategy can be useful to tackle fears which crop up repeatedly.

Generalised Anxiety Problems. The client with fears of specific situations may have similar fears each time he faces the situation. However, the client with general worries is likely to have a whole range of fears, and the ABC form described in Chapters 3 (Figure 1) and 6 (Figure 2) is useful in this instance. The form is used for the client to record and practise challenging his anxious thinking. On the record form, the client records any occasion when he feels anxious: he writes down his anxious thoughts, and then works out challenges to his negative thinking and some realistic alternative thoughts. After a few weeks of using this form, the client will find that he is starting to challenge negative thoughts automatically.

An imagery exercise which is also useful for clients with general worries, is an exercise called 'time projection' (Lazarus, 1981). Often when a client has a dread of something happening, he cannot see life beyond that event; for example, the student who dreads failing his examinations and to whom this seems the end of the world. Similarly, the person who dreads the break-up of a personal relationship, and who cannot see any future for himself. For the time projection method, the counsellor gets the client to imagine himself perhaps two or three years hence, and he asks the client what he thinks he would be doing and feeling then. Supposing a client's relationship did fail: in two or three years time he is likely to have got over his depressed feelings about the relationship, and he may well be enjoying a new relationship. Helping the client to see these possibilities will reduce his hopelessness, and help him to see that he will adjust to the dreaded event, and that the future may not unfold in the bleak way that he thinks.

Finally, when a client has a number of worries which tend to be in the back of his mind most of the day, it can be useful to introduce the idea of 'worry periods'. The client with a generalised anxiety problem spends long periods ruminating about problems, but the time spent worrying is rarely spent constructively. The idea of worry periods is for the client to designate a certain time period each day – perhaps half an hour – to sit down and make a concerted attempt to problem-solve worries and dispute negative thinking. At other times of the day, if the client starts to worry about something, he notes what the worry was and then tries to push it out of his mind until the worry period. The aim is to cut down on aimless worrying and to replace it with short periods of constructive problem-solving.

Behavioural Aspects of Anxiety
Avoidance is a very common feature of anxiety problems, and the client's restricted lifestyle as a result of avoidance is often what leads a client to seek help. Clients with agoraphobia, social anxiety or simple phobias tend to avoid specific situations such as shops, meeting people or animals. However, the anxious person may also avoid doing things which produce anxiety, such as writing a difficult letter or making a decision. The client may try to ignore a problem situation, hoping that it will go away. An extreme case in which a client avoided facing up to a problem was a client whose wife stayed out all night, every night for over two years, and he never even asked her where she went, for fear of what he might find out.

Helping a client to counter his avoidance is an important part of CBC with the anxious client. First, the counsellor needs to identify the negative beliefs that underly the avoidance. The most common reasons for avoidance are fear of becoming anxious, fear of negative evaluation by others, and fear of failure. Once the counsellor has identified the self-defeating beliefs and helped the client to challenge them verbally, she helps the client to set-up behavioural tasks to challenge the beliefs behaviourally. These tasks involve the client gradually overcoming his avoidance (general methods of setting up behavioural tasks were described in detail in Chapter 6).

Graded Exposure. The main behavioural method of helping the anxious client to overcome his avoidance is called 'graded exposure' (derived from Wolpe, 1958). This is especially useful with clients with agoraphobia, social phobia and simple phobias, where the client avoids specific situations.

In graded exposure, the counsellor and client first put together a list of the situations that the client avoids. The counsellor can assist the client to identify situations by asking, 'What things would you be doing if you didn't have this anxiety problem: what things would you be doing which you are not doing now?' A situation is only entered on the list if the client wishes to make a goal of going into that situation.

After the list has been put together, the client then rates the degree of difficulty which he thinks he would experience when going into each situation. The client rates the degree of difficulty on a scale from 0–100, where a score of '0' would mean 'no difficulty' and a score of '100' would mean 'the most difficult possible'. If the client gives several situations the same score, for example '100', the counsellor asks the client to put these situations into order of difficulty, and the scores are revised accordingly. Included in the list may be different scores for the client going into the situation alone or accompanied, or different scores for going into the situation under different circumstances – for example, going into a public house on a quiet lunch-time versus on a Saturday evening.

Once the ratings have been completed, the counsellor and client put the situations into order of difficulty, and it is helpful if the counsellor gives the client a copy of this list to work from. The client and counsellor then choose one or two of the easier situations, and tasks are decided which involve the client going into these easier situations. When the client has practised going into these situations several times and can do so with reasonable ease, he then moves onto more difficult situations. This continues until all the situations have been mastered, or the client has achieved as much as he can.

The guiding principle when setting the tasks is that the client needs to experience some anxiety when he enters the situation, but not an overwhelming degree of anxiety (further details about how to prepare clients for behavioural tasks, and dealing with blocks to progress, are given in Chapter 6). After entering the situation, the client tries to remain in the situation until he feels calmer, and he needs to verbally challenge his negative thinking whilst in the situation. On continuing to enter the feared situation on a number of occasions, the client will gradually disprove for himself the self-defeating beliefs that led to his avoidance of the situation.

Somatic Aspects of Anxiety
Over-Breathing. Reference was made earlier in this chapter to the fact that when some clients have a panic attack, they start over-breathing. This over-breathing, or hyperventilation, reduces the level of carbon-dioxide in the blood and produces lightheadedness, dizziness, quickened heart beat and tingling sensations (Clark et al., 1985). The client usually interprets these unpleasant feelings as meaning he is further losing control, and he becomes even more anxious.

Feeling breathless is a common symptom of anxiety, and this can easily lead to over-breathing. Sometimes a client over-breathes by taking rapid shallow breaths, or sometimes by taking large gulps of air in big sighs.

The over-breathing can be dealt with by teaching the client to modify his breathing, and Clark et al. (1985) have outlined the following procedures for doing this. To begin with, it is necessary to ascertain carefully whether or not the client is over-breathing. A useful method for checking this is to get the client to over-breathe deliberately for a minute or two. The counsellor then asks the client to compare the resulting sensations with what he experiences when he is anxious. If the experience is similar, this is a good clue that the client is over-breathing. She then explains to the client the likely role of breathing in his panic attacks.

A useful method of reducing the over-breathing is by means of breathing exercises. The client slows down his breathing by counting 'one, two, three' as he inhales, and 'four, five, six' as he exhales, such that he breathes in and out on a six-second cycle. The breaths should be fairly shallow, and the breathing is further slowed down by breathing through the nose. If the client follows this procedure as soon as he notices the first signs of over-breathing, the symptoms are likely to subside after two or three minutes.

In order for the client to be able to use this breathing method when he become anxious, he needs to practise it for five to ten minutes each day until he can carry it out with ease. A tape-recording of counting can be used to help the client to pace his breathing. For the final part of the training, the counsellor asks the client to deliberately over-breathe for a brief time (10–30 seconds) and then practise slowing his breathing by the counting method. By doing this practice in the counselling session, the client both learns the method and builds up confidence in his ability to control the over-breathing. He then tries to slow his breathing using the counting method whenever he starts to over-breathe.

A distressing feature of over-breathing which hampers progress is that the hyperventilating person feels breathless as if he were not breathing enough (when he is actually breathing too much). The client therefore needs to ignore the breathless feelings and keep encouraging himself to slow his breathing.

When a client starts to panic, he tends to interpret his symptoms as meaning that there is something seriously physically wrong with him. Teaching a client who hyperventilates about the role of breathing in his panics, helps the client to attribute his symptoms to the over-breathing rather than to some physical disaster. This helps to lessen the client's anxiety about his anxiety symptoms and, in turn, makes a full-blown panic less likely. Moreover, teaching the client a method to deal with the hyperventilation helps the client to feel more in control of his anxiety, and more capable of coping with it.

Relaxation. Physical tension is a common feature of anxiety problems, and this can be relieved by means of relaxation methods. Helping the client to relax himself physically enables the client to be less anxious, and being calmer also makes it easier for him to think in a less anxious way.

Relaxation is a skill which is usually taught by means of a series of exercises. The most common form of exercises are those derived from Jacobsen (1938) in which the client systematically relaxes and tenses groups of muscles throughout the body. Alternative forms of exercise include thinking relaxing imagery (for example, a country-side scene) or concentrating on counting breaths.

The relaxation exercises can be recorded onto an audiotape for the client to practise at home. The client practises the exercises each day, either sitting in an armchair or lying on the bed. The client should avoid going to sleep during the exercises, for the aim of them is to teach him to be relaxed while awake. After practising the relaxation exercises for two or three weeks, the client will start to develop the skill of relaxing.

The next step is for the client to identify times in the day when he starts to become tense, and then to carry out a quick relaxation procedure. For quick relaxation, the client takes some slow deep breaths and mentally works through his body, relaxing each set of muscles. As a result of his practice carrying out the full relaxation method, he will find that he is able to do this. Gradually, the client starts to notice his physical tension sooner, and is able to deal with it more effectively.

However, the relaxation not only reduces the client's level of tension; the fact that the client knows that he can use relaxation to help control his anxiety, helps to boost his confidence that he can cope with the anxiety-provoking situation. Concentrating on relaxation when in difficult situations can also serve a useful function by distracting the client away from anxious thinking.

Anxiety is often a client's major problem. Anxiety, however, may also be a secondary feature of other major difficulties, such as depression.

8 Depression

The term 'depression' can be used to refer to a syndrome or a mood state. Many people get periods of depressed or low mood, but this is different to depression the syndrome, which consists of a whole range of symptoms which form a pattern.

The symptoms of depression can be divided into the following categories (Beck et al., 1979):

Motivational: apathy, loss of energy and interest;
Affective: depressed mood, guilt, anxiety, anger;
Behavioural: decreased activity, reduced coping, social skills deficits;
Cognitive: negative thinking, indecisiveness, poor concentration;
Biological: sleep disturbance, loss of appetite, decreased sexual interest.

Negative thinking is usually a prominent part of depression, and the depressed person thinks negatively about his ongoing experiences, the future and himself (Beck, 1970). The depressed person is unhappy with his life situation, feels unable to alter the situation, and cannot see how things could change in the future. Moreover, the content of the depressed person's negative thinking tends to centre on the theme of loss or a failure to achieve a valued goal. For example, a client may be depressed about the break-up of his marriage (a loss) or about his poor marital relationship (failure to achieve a valued goal).

The motivational, affective and behavioural symptoms can usually be linked to specific types of negative thinking. For example:

Apathy: 'What's the point', 'It's not worth trying';
Depressed mood: 'I'll never find another girlfriend like her';
Reduced coping: 'I just can't cope with it any more'.

The symptoms that the depressed person experiences can seem to him to be a whole collection of problems to be overcome. It can therefore be helpful to inform the client that his symptoms are features of depression and that they will reduce as his depression lifts. It can reduce the immensity of the whole problem in the client's mind to reattribute the collection of symptoms to one single problem – namely depression. It will also help the client not to get so depressed about his symptoms because the counsellor can explain that anyone who gets depressed will, for example, not feel like sex. Therefore his reduced sex drive is not something to get unduly worried about because it is something that is likely to come and go with the depression.

Guilt
Guilt is a common feature of depression, and this topic is dealt with in detail in Chapter 9. Briefly, normal guilt occurs when a person thinks that he has done something wrong, and pathological guilt occurs when a person adds to this the belief that as a result he is a bad person. Self-punishment is an extension of pathological guilt and occurs when the person draws the further conclusion that because he is a bad person, he deserves punishment. Self-blame is the most common form of self-punishment in depressed people. For example, a depressed client may blame himself entirely for problems in his relationship despite the fact that his partner may be acting quite unreasonably. In some cases, the depressed person may take the self-blame further and try to cause himself physical pain as a way of punishing himself (for example, cutting at the wrists).

Suicidal Behaviour
Suicide and attempted suicide may be the result of extreme hopelessness – when the client thinks that his life is unbearable and he cannot see any possibility of the situation changing in the future. Alternatively, suicidal behaviour may be a client's cry for help to those about him. Thirdly, suicidal behaviour may be an act of hostility to punish significant others in the client's life. Of course, the suicidal person may have a mixture of these thoughts and motivations, and methods of dealing with these are described later in the chapter.

Aims of Working with the Depressed Client
In the case of the syndrome of depression, the aim of CBC is to identify and list the various symptoms the client is experiencing and to tackle them one at a time (for example, inactivity, hopelessness, depressed mood). As regards the client's mood, the client who realistically appraises problems, rather than viewing problems in catastophic terms, will tend to feel sad rather than depressed about his problems. If the client is feeling sad rather than depressed, he is also less likely to be paralysed by his problems, and is more likely to face up to them and to try to deal with them.

Specific Strategies for Working with Depressed Clients

Inactivity and Apathy
A common symptom of more severely depressed clients is inactivity and lack of drive, and it is often useful to start tackling these problems near the beginning of counselling. This is for a number of reasons. First, activity planning is one of the most effective ways of helping a client to overcome apathy and lift mood. Second, until his mood has lifted somewhat, the more severely depressed client may have difficulty concentrating adequately to participate in the verbal challenging of his negative thinking. Finally, starting to tackle the client's motivational difficulty through the activity planning, will aid the client's motivation to work on other aspects of his depression.

The depressed person's inactivity often results from negative thinking such as 'It's a waste of time doing anything', or 'I can't do it – it's too difficult'. Typically, the problem is compounded by the client becoming depressed about his inactivity, and the fact that he finds it difficult to carry out tasks which he used to do without thinking, before he became depressed. Another factor is that the depressed client who does little is likely to spend most of his time ruminating. He therefore becomes more depressed because of the large amount of time he is spending thinking negatively. Moreover, because the inactive client is doing little, he gets little opportunity to gain any sense of pleasure from doing things. This loss of pleasurable activity results in low mood and a further decrease in motivation. Once this process has started, the depressed client fails to gain pleasure out of activities which were once pleasurable (Costello, 1972).

Activity Planning
A useful method for dealing with apathy and inactivity is to help the client to make a plan of activities – especially pleasurable ones. The method described in Figure 3 is based upon the work of Beck et al. (1979). It is easier for the client to become more active if he has a plan of what to do and when. The plan takes away the problem of indecision about what to do, and completing the plan adds an extra reason for doing things.

Depending on how depressed he is, the client may at first need quite a lot of help to make a plan of activities. For most clients it will be sufficient to make a plan for one day's tasks in order for the client to learn what to do. The plan is completed by entering an activity for each time slot on an activity chart as shown in Figure 3. (The time slots can be altered to suit the varying day-time hours of clients.)

WEEKLY ACTIVITY CHART

	Monday	Tuesday	Wednesday	Thursday	Friday	Saturday	Sunday
8–9	breakfast	breakfast	breakfast	breakfast	breakfast	breakfast	bed
9–10	paper/radio	magazine/radio	paper/radio	magazine/radio	paper/radio	paper/radio	breakfast
10–11	vacuum & dust	clean kitchen	water plants	clean bathroom & toilet	vacuum & dust	shopping	bath
11–12	laundry	see friend	ironing	laundry	see friend	shopping	clearing up
12–1	lunch	lunch	lunch	lunch	lunch	prepare lunch	prepare lunch
1–2	T.V.	T.V.	T.V.	T.V.	T.V.	lunch	lunch
2–3	shopping	mending	shopping	visit mother	shopping	see mother	walk with husband
3–4	tidy up rest	tidy up rest	tidy up rest	tidy up rest	tidy up rest	rest	rest
4–5	prepare tea	prepare tea	prepare tea	prepare tea	prepare tea	prepare tea	prepare tea
5–6	tea	tea	tea	tea	tea	tea	tea
6–7	T.V.	T.V. knitting	ring mother	T.V.	T.V. knitting	T.V.	ring mother
7–8	T.V.	bath	T.V.	T.V.	T.V.	pub	T.V.
8–12	T.V./bed	T.V./bed	T.V./bed	T.V./bed	T.V./bed	pub/bed	T.V./bed

Figure 3 Chart for activity planning

A major consideration in choosing tasks is to make them achievable (for example, reading for fifteen minutes rather than reading a whole novel!). The tasks can also be graded, with the client first completing very simple activities and progressing onto more demanding tasks. The example of a plan given in Figure 3 involves quite intensive activity, and how full a plan is made will depend upon the client's level of activity prior to the activity planning (the aim is to build up activity slowly).

Another consideration in making the plan is to incorporate a number of pleasurable activities. If the client says that he does not enjoy anything at the moment, choose activities which the client used to enjoy. It is necessary to stress the inclusion of pleasurable activities because some clients think that they do not deserve to do 'nice' things because they are not doing anything worthwhile.

Within the client's plan of activities needs to be included a time for the client to plan the following day's activities. If the client finds it difficult to think up a plan, his partner or friend can be enlisted to help. It can also help if the client has a list of potential activities to select from, as this reduces the difficulty of choosing activities. It is also necessary to stress that the plan is a guide and need not be rigidly adhered to, and also that the client should not give up making a plan just because he has not kept to it for a day or two.

Finally, as with the setting of any therapeutic task, it is worth exploring the client's thoughts about the task and any obstacles that he can foresee. The counsellor can then problem-solve these obstacles with the client (see Chapter 6 for a description of common blocks to progress).

Cognitive Change through Activity Planning

Carrying out an activity plan can help the client to overcome his helplessness by teaching him that he *can* control events in his life and make changes. However, it is important that the client recognises his achievement, rather than dismisses his efforts. This is where Beck et al.'s (1979) idea of mastery and pleasure ratings is of value. For this, the counsellor asks the client to rate the degree of pleasure and the degree of achievement he has obtained from the activities he has completed. The ratings are made on a ten point scale, where 'P0' means he gained no pleasure from the activity and a score of 'P10' indicates extreme pleasure. Similarly, ratings would be made for achievement on a scale running from 'A0' to 'A10'. The ratings can be recorded beside the description of the activity on the activity chart.

Achievement Ratings. A problem of depressed people is that they often focus on what they are *not* doing or *not* managing rather than on what they *are* managing to do. In addition, depressed people tend to dismiss their achievements by always thinking how much easier they used to be able to do things before they became depressed. In order to counteract this, the counsellor stresses that when the client rates his achievement in carrying out an activity, he needs to take into account how he is feeling and how difficult it is to make himself do the activity.

It can often help to give the client an example to illustrate this point. For instance, is it more of an achievement for a person to pass an examination who has great difficulty in learning the material, or for another to pass the exam who finds the work very easy? Most people will agree that it is more of an achievement for the person who has to struggle to pass the examination. This is analogous to the client's situation where he is not making allowances for the fact that it is difficult for a depressed person to do even simple activities. An alternative illustration is to ask the client to rate the degree of achievement involved in getting up, when a person wakes up feeling fresh and on top of the world, compared to when the person wakes up feeling tired and lacking in energy. Again the client will see that it is more of an achievement to get up if a person really does not feel like doing so. The aim of these analogies is to teach the client to make allowances for his depression when he rates the achievement of his activities. Through recognising his achievements, the client will build up his own confidence, rather than knocking it down, as the depressed person tends to do.

Pleasure Ratings. Apart from dismissing the value of what he does, the depressed person also tends to dismiss the enjoyment that he has gained from activities. The person may think that he does not enjoy anything; yet this is usually found to be untrue when the client starts to record pleasure ratings (although the levels of enjoyment may be low).

The depressed client is likely to conclude that if he gets little enjoyment out of an activity, then the activity is not worth doing. However, the result of thinking this way is that the client does less and less, and gets little opportunity to gain enjoyment. If the client remains active and obtains at least some satisfaction out of activities, he is likely to maintain a higher level of motivation.

Pleasure ratings are useful when the client thinks negatively about doing things, because the ratings focus the client's attention on the pleasure that he does get from activities. One way in which the counsellor can help the client to see that carrying out activities is worthwhile, is to ask the client how much enjoyment he would get if he did nothing. The answer is obviously that he would not have obtained any pleasure at all. The client may then see that it is better to get a little enjoyment than to get none at all. The counsellor can also point out the positive benefit that gaining even a little enjoyment will encourage the client to do more, and consequently gain more enjoyment.

A further use of pleasure ratings is when a client looks back on a day with a negative bias and concludes that he has felt bad all day. Again, the ratings can help by pointing out to the client the fact that, at certain times in the day, he may have felt much better than at other times.

A final point is that achievement and pleasure ratings are not only useful for testing the client's conclusions, but are also useful for testing the client's negative predictions about his activities. For example, the client may be willing to try to do some activities, yet predict that he would not enjoy them. The ratings can be used to test this prediction. Similarly, the client may predict that he cannot do anything, yet find that he is able to do things with the help of an activity plan.

Awareness of the Effect of Negative Thinking on Mood
Before a client learns to challenge his own negative thinking, he needs to become aware of the effects of his negative thinking on his mood and behaviour. Particularly useful for this purpose, is the mood induction procedure described in detail in Chapter 4. The counsellor first identifies a chain of negative inferences and evaluations which the client makes in response to a situation, and by the end of this procedure the client's mood has usually been lowered. Then, she proceeds to help the client to generate more helpful alternatives for each of the negative thoughts, and by the end of this procedure the client's mood rises again. The difference in mood is emphasised by getting the client to rate his mood after identifying the negative thinking, and again after generating the more realistic alternative thoughts. The client can then see quite easily that the changes in his mood were the result of changes in his thinking about the situation.

Depression about Depression
Just as anxious clients become anxious about their anxiety symptoms, so depressed clients get depressed about their depressive symptoms. For example, the depressed person may get depressed about his lack of energy and feeling unsociable, and this makes him all the more depressed (particularly if he starts to blame himself for being 'lazy' and 'useless'). Depression about depression can often be the major factor involved in keeping someone depressed, and this should be a point of focus early on in CBC.

Negative Self-Evaluations

Negative self-evaluations are often triggered when the client thinks that he has made a mistake, done something stupid, or shown a weakness, by getting depressed, for instance. The client then concludes that he is a failure, is stupid, useless or worthless. The mistake that clients make when they evaluate themselves in this way, is to over-generalise from a single thing about themselves which they dislike, to making broad statements which devalue themselves as a whole person. For example, a client who failed to complete a homework assignment thought she was a 'failure', saying, 'I can't even do a simple task like this' (see the section on 'evaluations' in Chapter 3).

Whenever a client makes sweeping negative self-evaluations, the aim is to teach him that however frequently he makes mistakes or fails at things, this cannot mean he is a failure as a person. The counsellor tries to get the client to rate his behaviour rather than make invalid over-generalisations about himself. Take, for example, the client who thinks that he is a failure because his relationship has failed. The counsellor would aim to help the client to see that even if the relationship did fail solely as a result of his behaviour (an unlikely situation), this only means that he failed at this relationship and nothing more. It cannot mean that *he* is a failure as a person. The general aim is for the client to accept himself as a fallible human being, including his weaknesses and mistakes.

A useful way to illustrate the errors in the client's negative self-evaluations is to draw three circles on a sheet of paper, representing the person who is a 'complete failure', the person who is 'perfect', and the person who is 'human' (see Figure 4). Fill the circle representing the 'failure' with crosses to indicate that every single thing he does fails. Next, the circle representing the 'perfect person' is filled with small circles, indicating that everything he does is good and successful. Lastly, the circle representing the ordinary person who is 'human' is filled with a mixture of circles and crosses, indicating that he experiences both success and failure.

The counsellor first asks the client whether he fits the 'failure' diagram. In other words, does he actually fail at *everything* he does? (If he fails at everything, how did he manage to get to the counselling session?) The client is likely to respond to this question by agreeing that he does not fit this description. The counsellor then moves on to the diagram of the 'perfect' person and asks the client whether he fits this description – and the client will normally say 'no'. Finally, she asks the client what he would call the person with the mixture of circles and crosses (that is, a mixture of successes and failures). The client is likely to say something to the effect that this person is 'human' or an 'ordinary person'. The counsellor then asks the client

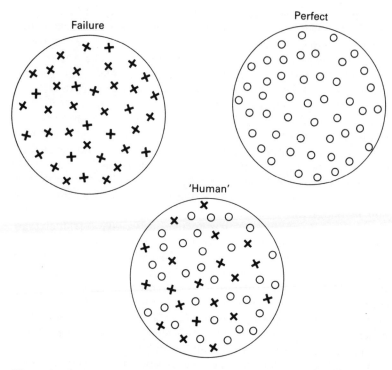

Figure 4   *Diagrams for use when showing to clients the invalid nature of global, negative self-evaluations*

whether he thinks he fits this description, and the client will usually indicate his agreement. By means of the diagrams, she steers the client towards seeing that he and everyone else fits the 'fallible human being' category. Thus, it is clearly an error for the client to call himself a 'failure' for failing at something (or even for failing at lots of things).

The type of realistic alternative thinking that the counsellor would encourage would be: 'I'll try to avoid that mistake next time, but I'm just a human being who makes mistakes, and that's the way it is.' For example, a client who thinks that he is a failure because his marriage ended might learn to say to himself something like, 'Well, I did fail to keep my marriage going, but that does not mean that I am a failure in every way. I am perfectly competent in some ways. I made some serious mistakes, but that is just too bad.'

It is worth noting that global negative self-evaluations are linked with the client's demanding thinking such as: 'I must not act stupidly' or 'I must not show weakness'. It follows that if the client *must not* behave stupidly or weakly, then it is 'awful' if he does. Furthermore, the client concludes that *he* must be 'awful' for acting in this 'awful' way.

Suicidal Thinking
Suicide is, of course, always a danger with the depressed person, and the counsellor needs to be on the lookout for any direct or indirect clues about suicidal intentions that the client has. The client may speak quite openly about his suicidal intent, or his feelings may be revealed less obviously in comments such as 'I can't stand it any more' or 'it's no use going on'. Alternatively, suicidal intent may become apparent from the client's actions, such as being suddenly concerned to make a will, tidying up financial arrangements, or acting secretively.

Once the counsellor has become aware of the client's suicidal thinking, she should encourage a full discussion in order to explore how seriously suicide is being considered. Factors to be explored include whether the client has actually made any definite plans to kill himself or has decided how he would do it. Moreover, whether the client has access to ways of killing himself, such as being in possession of lethal doses of tablets. If the person is considered to be at risk it might well be necessary to contact the person's family or friends and other health professionals who are involved with that person, if possible, with the client's permission. The counsellor may also wish to keep in telephone contact with the person between sessions.

It is worth noting that even low suicidal intent may be lethal. The client, for example, may take an overdose of medication in the belief that his partner will find him, but when the partner is delayed returning home the client dies. The lesson is therefore that all suicidal intent needs to be taken seriously.

Two main reasons for suicidal thinking and behaviour have been identified by Beck et al. (1979). The first is to do with a client's hopelessness and occurs when the client reaches a stage where he cannot see any way out of his problems or any end to his distress, and he comes to the conclusion that he cannot stand his distress any longer. Death may even seem an attractive prospect for it offers the client relief from his emotional suffering. For example, one client tried to kill himself because his wife did not love him, and he thought he could not stand living without this love. In other cases, the client may see himself as an awful burden on other people and think that other people would be better off without him.

The second set of reasons for suicidal thinking and behaviour concerns a client's attempts to manipulate his environment in some way. For example, the suicide attempt may aim to bring back a loved one, make others realise that help is needed, get revenge, or even to get into hospital. In these cases, the attempt can be seen as a maladaptive coping strategy, and the counsellor needs to ask herself 'What problem is the client trying to solve?' or 'What message is the client trying to give?' One young client lived in a family situation where her mother was out every night, and her father was very withdrawn and had a long-term problem with depression. She reported that she took an overdose of medication because she felt it was the only way she could get her parents to take notice of her.

Finally, it is important to note that a client is likely to have a mixture of reasons for being suicidal, and a careful analysis of his motives is necessary. The client is also likely to be more aware of some feelings than others, and to find it easier to admit to feelings such as hopelessness rather than hostility and revenge.

Strategies for Dealing with Suicidal Thinking. Once a client's hopeless thinking has been identified, it can be tackled using the various methods of challenging beliefs described in Chapters 3 and 5. In particular, it is useful to get the client to weigh up the advantages and disadvantages of living, for the suicidal person often ignores the positive factors in his life and can only see the negative. The client will find it difficult to identify positive factors about his life, and it is therefore helpful for the client and counsellor to review the various aspects of life which may be positive factors (such as physical health, home, family, friends, work, interests, skills and so on). It may also help to encourage the client to identify things which used to give meaning to his life before he became depressed, and which could give meaning in the future.

As regards the disadvantages of living (or reasons for dying) identified by the client, it is often useful to evaluate with the client the evidence that these are going to be permanent factors in his life. For example, the client whose partner has left him may think that he will never find another partner and that he will never be happy again. The second conclusion, in particular, is likely to be false and would be worth challenging with the client.

An additional approach is to tackle the client's thinking that he 'cannot stand' feeling as he does. By disputing the client's belief that he 'cannot stand' his distress, the counsellor helps the client to re-evaluate the distress as extremely uncomfortable, but bearable (see the section on 'blocks to the completion of homework tasks' in Chapter 6).

Whenever a client's suicidal behaviour is an attempt to create changes in other people, it is helpful to consider with the client more adaptive ways of coping with his problems. This may involve teaching the client and those around him a variety of skills, including problem-solving skills, communication skills or social skills (see Chapter 5 for a summary of these methods). For example, when one sixteen-year-old client attempted suicide to draw her parent's attention to her, one parent never spoke a word to her about the attempt and the reaction of the other parent was that lots of teenage girls attempted suicide. In this case, work with the whole family was necessary to help the daughter to communicate her needs more effectively and to help the family to listen to her and to take more account of her.

Pitfalls in CBC with Depressed People

There are a few common pitfalls in carrying out CBC which occur particularly in CBC with depressed people. Each pitfall is described briefly and is followed by suggestions about how to deal with the situation.

Negativity about the Counselling
It is not surprising that if a depressed client has a negative perspective about his life and experiences, he will also tend to take a gloomy view about the counselling and the counsellor. Therefore, as illustrated throughout Chapters 2 to 4, it is important to give permission and time for the client to give the counsellor feedback concerning the counselling. This can be carried out by a simple check at the end of each counselling session when the counsellor asks what the client has found to be useful or upsetting or unhelpful.

A lack of motivation is a central feature of depression, and so the client is also likely to view homework tasks in a negative light. He may not believe that the task could help him, or may think that the task is too difficult. Again the counsellor needs to identify and gently challenge such negative thinking (see the section on 'blocks to the completion of homework tasks' in Chapter 6).

Confronting the Client with Positive Information too Quickly
Sometimes a depressed person's negative perception of things seems so fixed that it appears as if the person is deliberately resisting any positive information about his situation. When this happens, the dialogue may take the form of 'Yes, it is/No, it isn't' or the client repeatedly gives 'Yes-buts'. If the counsellor finds herself in this position, then it probably means that she is pressing positive evidence on the client too quickly or too didactically. It is important to get clients to recognise the positive aspects of their experiences themselves by carrying out a collaborative review of the evidence.

Another useful strategy for dealing with resistance to positive evidence is to postpone the verbal challenging of negative thinking in the counselling session, and instead for the client and counsellor to work out together a behavioural experiment which will test the negative thinking.

Colluding with the Client's Negative Thinking
When clients have serious problems in their lives, it is easy for the counsellor to collude with the client's negatively distorted view of the world, and to agree that things really are awful for that person. However, if the counsellor holds fast in applying the CBC model she will find the person who is depressed will almost certainly have an unrealistically negative view of his life, even if he has a number of objectively serious losses or problems with which to contend.

Moreover, it is important to bear in mind that just because things are bad for the person at the time, this does not mean that things must be like this forever. Another thought to bear in mind is that a large number of people experience very serious problems and losses without becoming depressed, and it is clearly possible to take a more adaptive view of such problems.

With many depressed clients, a breakthrough occurs as they gradually realise that their depressing view of reality is not necessarily correct and that things may well be better than they seem. This insight comes when the client has had a few successful experiences of modifying his own thinking.

Someone who is clinically depressed may experience a range of dysfunctional emotions, and in the last two chapters we have focused upon anxiety problems and depressed mood. In the next chapter, the topics of anger, guilt and shame are considered in their own right, but these are also relevant to the counselling of the depressed person.

9 Shame, Guilt and Anger

Shame, guilt and anger are often experienced by clients as part of anxiety problems, depression and other difficulties. Clients may also seek counselling help specifically for problems with shame, guilt and anger, particularly in the case of anger problems.

Shame and Embarrassment

The people who experience a lot of shame and embarrassment are those who are particularly sensitive about what other people think about them (Edelmann, 1987). Shame and embarrassment are therefore particularly prominent in people with social anxiety. A person experiences shame when he thinks he has been revealed to be weak, inferior or incompetent by being observed to break some social rule. Shame is triggered when (a) others observe a person breaking a social rule, (b) the person infers that those watching him are making negative evaluations about what he has done, and (c) the person applies these negative evaluations to himself.

For example, one client felt ashamed about her anxiety problem and therefore did not tell her husband or anyone else that she was seeking help. She believed that her family, friends and work colleagues would ridicule her for having the problem, and she thought that she was bad for being so weak. Note from this example, that the negative evaluation from others which leads to shame need not actually happen, but may simply be inferred.

Embarrassment can be viewed as a milder form of shame: the same type of thinking processes occur, but the personal weakness is regarded by the person as less serious than that which triggers shame (Dryden, 1987). For example, a person might experience embarrassment if he spilt some coffee but shame if he was caught out telling a lie. Therefore, both shame and embarrassment result when the person agrees with the negative evaluations he infers that others have made about him. Self-devaluation is therefore central to shame and embarrassment.

When a person is feeling ashamed or embarrassed, he usually experiences an intense desire to remove himself from the public view. This is achieved by looking down and avoiding eye contact, or by withdrawing from the situation. The person may well wish that 'the ground would swallow him up'. As Dryden (1987) notes, the embarrassed person may paradoxically draw more attention to himself by blushing or becoming agitated. The feeling of shame and embarrassment may last for quite a long time, and the problem may be compounded by 'I can't stand it' thinking, such as in the case of the person who says 'I could never face them again after that.' This way of thinking leads to avoidance and further difficulties.

A client's shame about his difficulties can be a major block to progress, even where shame is secondary to the client's main problem. As a result of shame about his problems, a client will sometimes hold back from telling the counsellor the whole story about his problems. For example, shame prevented one client for a long time from admitting to an experience when her father had sexually interfered with her. A common indication of a client's shame about his difficulties is when he avoids telling his partner, family or friends about seeking counselling help. A client may also drop out of treatment or avoid counselling as a result of shame. This can therefore be an important emotional disturbance to address in the early stages of counselling.

Regret as an Alternative to Shame

Dryden (1987) suggests that regret is an adaptive alternative to shame and embarrassment. When regretful, a person is sorry about his behaviour or weakness, but he does not devalue himself because of it. He regrets his action but does not criticise himself as a whole person (that was a stupid action, but that does not mean that I am a stupid person). The person who feels regret will still try to avoid repeating the mistake, but is less likely than the person who feels ashamed to avoid facing the same social situation again.

A further aim is for the client who regrets an action to evaluate the consequences of his action realistically, and to avoid 'awfulising' about what happened.

Strategies for Working with Clients with Shame Problems

Shame can be tackled in the same way as other emotional problems by verbally disputing the logicality of the client's self-devaluation, and by setting up behavioural experiments to test out the client's beliefs. In Chapter 7 we pointed out that these experiments are called 'shame-attacking exercises' in rational-emotive therapy, where the client deliberately does something which is likely to attract disapproval or rejection (avoiding tasks with potentially serious negative consequences for the client or other people). By deliberately doing something that he finds 'shameful', the client can learn that he does not need others' approval to remain a worthwhile person and this will help him to overcome his fear of disapproval (Wessler and Wessler, 1980).

For example, one client felt ashamed at the prospect of 'creating a scene' at the cinema or theatre, if he became anxious and had to leave in the middle of the film or performance. His shame-attacking exercise was to go to the cinema and theatre and to leave his seat in the middle of the performance and return to it a few minutes later. While doing this, the client also verbally challenged his shameful beliefs by telling himself that he was not a bad person for inconveniencing the other members of the audience, and that it was not disastrous if people did glare at him or pass a negative comment.

Another client was extremely sensitive about 'saying something stupid' in front of people. If she said anything which received a negative or even neutral response from her work colleagues, she would 'feel stupid' and experience embarrassment. An important part of helping this client was to enable her to realise that even if she did say something stupid, this could not mean that she was a stupid person. In addition, the counsellor helped the client to identify more accurately whether or not people were implying that she was stupid.

When a client is ashamed about his problems, the fact that the counsellor is listening to his problems without criticising him can be helpful. However, it is easy for the client to see her as a special case – a person whom the client would expect to show understanding of his problem. A useful task to overcome the shame about the problem is for the client to tell a relative or friend about his problem, whilst at the same time challenging his shameful beliefs.

Guilt

Guilt is another emotion commonly experienced by depressed and anxious clients. Guilt occurs when a person thinks he has done something morally wrong; he has violated his own standards or moral code. This is normal guilt. However, the evaluation that he is guilty of doing something wrong is not sufficient to make the person feel extremely distressed. For this to occur he has also to evaluate that he is guilty of being a bad person because of what he has done. This is pathological guilt. So, a woman who feels depressed about an abortion is not only saying that she thinks she has done wrong, but also that she is an unworthy person because of it.

When a person feels pathological guilt, he may react in a number of ways which compound his problems. Several such maladaptive 'action tendencies' have been identified by Dryden (1987). First, the client may try to mend the wrong in unproductive ways, such as by desperately begging forgiveness. At the same time, the client will often loathe himself for acting in this degrading way.

Second, the person may resort to self-punishment and either be-rate himself for what he has done or even actually physically harm himself. The reasoning followed by the client is that he has done something awful, he is therefore an awful person, and therefore deserves punishment. This kind of thinking can, of course, have serious consequences, where a person inflicts injury upon himself; one client, for example, cut her wrist with scissors in order to punish herself for having sexual/religious obsessive thoughts.

As with anxiety and depression, a person who feels pathological guilt may try to drown or block out the feelings by use of drink or drugs. This, of course, may achieve short-term relief but creates its own problems in the long term.

A fourth way in which a person may react to pathological guilt is to try to avoid responsibility by making excuses or blaming others for what has happened. Blaming others is a common defence against guilt and this will be discussed in more detail in the section on anger.

A person who feels pathological guilt is often more preoccupied about achieving forgiveness from others or blaming himself than he is about how the mistake can be avoided in the future. The client will often make unrealistic promises that he will never do the thing again, without attempting to understand the factors which led him to act in that way. This makes it difficult for the person to learn from his errors and he often fails to keep his promises. A common pattern is where a husband may physically abuse his wife, the wife threatens to leave, the husband feels guilty and promises to be different but then gra-dually slips back into his old ways.

Quite often people who experience pathological guilt are very concerned about being 'selfish'. Since they interpret doing whatever *they* want to do as being selfish, they feel guilty much of the time. Paradoxically, this preoccupation with being unselfish often leads the person to be much more preoccupied with himself than someone who is assertive. The assertive person, who respects himself as well as others, is less self-centred and has more energy to devote to being sensitive to others' needs.

Normal Guilt as the Alternative to Pathological Guilt

Normal guilt is the realistic alternative to pathological guilt. Normal guilt occurs when a person is sorry that he has committed an immoral act, and this guilt will motivate the person not to repeat the act. The main difference between normal and pathological guilt is that the normally guilty person is not damning himself as a bad person because of his behaviour, in the way that the pathologically guilty person is.

Strategies for Working with Clients with Guilt Problems

There are two main ways in which the CBC counsellor can tackle a client's guilt. She may either challenge the client's belief in the wrongfulness of what he has done, or challenge the client's negative self-evaluation for what he has done. Thus, if a man is feeling guilty about being unfaithful to his wife or for not letting his aged parent live with him, one approach to lessen his guilt would be to challenge the values underlying the guilt, that is, challenge whether these things are 'wrong'. However, these values are not necessarily maladaptive in themselves and form part of normal guilt. It is the second component of guilt which is maladaptive – the way in which the person is putting himself down as a bad person for acting in the way he did. The aim in CBC is therefore for the guilty person to accept and forgive himself, and to realise that he is not bad person whatever he does. Realising this will help to provide the client with a general solution to his guilt.

This shift in attitude is achieved by getting the client to rate only his behaviour as bad, and to avoid global self-ratings (Ellis, 1977). For example, if a man is thinking he is awful because he has had an affair outside of his marriage, he might instead tell himself that he may have committed an immoral act, but that this does not make him a bad person.

In addition to challenging the self-damning aspect of pathological guilt, the counsellor may also challenge the client's 'awfulising' about what he has done. Take, for example, the client who felt very guilty if she ever said no to her husband's sexual advances. She thought that this might have some terribly damaging effect on him. When she evaluated the evidence for her conclusion, she decided that perhaps refusing her husband's sexual advances would not have such dire consequences as she had anticipated.

Finally, in some instances where the client's values are clearly unhealthy, the counsellor may decide to challenge these values. A common example is in assertiveness training where the counsellor is teaching the client to respect his own wishes and not always to put other people first. Consider, for example, a client who felt guilty about refusing her son's requests. One instance was when she felt guilty about refusing to let him borrow her car, although he was not legally allowed to drive it. This client's inability to set boundaries for her son, and lack of respect for her own wishes, created a number of problems. In this case, the counsellor disputed the client's belief that it was wrong to say 'no' to her son. In fact, there was clear evidence that her failure to say 'no' was having a detrimental effect on her son who was learning that, in order to get his own way, he had only to get angry or say something which would lead his mother to feel guilty.

The issue of changing the client's values is a tricky one. In the above example, most people would say that it was good and right for the mother to say no to her son without feeling guilty. However, there are many cases where the situation is less clear cut. Take, for example, a woman who feels guilty about having an abortion or a man who feels guilty about being sexually permissive. In such instances, opinions vary considerably about whether the behaviour of these individuals was 'right' or 'wrong'. The counsellor needs to be aware of her own values and avoid trying to press these upon the client. The key questions for the counsellor to bear in mind is whether or not the client's beliefs promote psychological well-being rather than whether they are morally right or wrong.

Anger

Frustrations are inevitable in life, as we are thwarted from getting what we want or when we do get what we don't want. This frustration may be a major event, such as not getting the promotion we thought we deserved, or a minor thing, such as a car pushing in front of us in a traffic queue. The source of this frustration may be other people, organisations, circumstances or, of course, ourselves. However, this frustration only turns to anger when we think that the frustrating situation absolutely should *not* have happened, and that it is awful that we have not got what we want (Wessler and Wessler, 1980). Anger becomes problematic when there is an absolute demand that what has happened should not have happened, and when the person damns the source of the frustration for causing the frustration. On the other hand, adaptive anger results from a preference that these frustrations do not occur.

An example of unhelpful anger was when one client became furious with her husband who thoughtlessly left her on her own at a party when she did not know many people. Her thinking was along the lines of: 'How could he leave me on my own? He should be more considerate. Damn him and damn his stupid friends. Just wait until he comes out with my friends and *he* doesn't know anyone.' Clearly, this damning attitude was not conducive to a constructive expression of her anger to her husband and this client spent a good proportion of her time in an angry state.

Sources of Anger

There are three main sources of anger. The first is when a person is blocked from achieving a valued goal, such as when a bus which a person usually catches to work fails to turn up. Dysfunctional anger results when the client demands to himself that the frustration absolutely should not have occurred.

The second common trigger for anger is through the breaking of personal rules (Beck, 1976). Common personal rules that an individual might hold would be that he should be treated politely, reasonably, and with fairness, consideration and respect. If the person strongly believes that he must always be treated in this way, he is likely to be very angry when people treat him rudely or unfairly. However, it is an unrealistic demand to expect that people must always treat others in this desirable way. It is more adaptive and realistic to have a strong preference to be treated in this way, but to accept that this will not always be the case.

A third type of anger, described by Dryden (1987) as self-defence anger, is where a person's self-esteem is threatened by the responses of another person or an organisation. This is where the person's anger protects him from negative self-evaluation. For example, if a team of people at work are told that their performance could be even better, one person might angrily respond that he *is* pulling his weight and doing a good job. The angry response protects him from the alternative conclusion in that person's mind that he is failing at his work and that this would be awful. If the client has the belief that to fail at something would mean he was a failure, then it seems to him that a person who is pointing out his failure on a task, is actually saying that he is a failure as a person. This explains the strength of this person's anger in response to criticism, and why it is so difficult for such a person to accept criticism.

The self-defence type of anger is common in people who are seen as 'defensive' or 'touchy', and those who are quick to blame others rather than accept responsibility themselves. These people find it difficult to take responsibility for errors because to them it would mean accepting that they were failures or worthless. The consequences of accepting responsibility for a mistake are therefore much more serious to a person who thinks in this way.

Consequences of Anger

When a person is angry, there is a tendency towards attacking or retaliating against the perceived cause of the frustration. This may of course be verbal or physical, or the anger may be shown in an indirect way, such as being awkward and unco-operative. One client would never show any annoyance with customers who were unpleasant to him; his way of getting back at them was to overcharge them. When a client's anger results from a demanding or damning way of thinking, he is more likely to respond in an aggressive or destructive manner.

Being angry frequently or over a long period of time is an unpleasant experience for most people. We talk about someone being 'consumed' with anger, and this is an apt phrase, for anger can 'eat away' at a person. As with other emotions, angry thinking can come to dominate a person's thoughts and prevent the person from enjoying life. There is also evidence that prolonged anger can lead to problems with high blood pressure (Chesney and Rosenman, 1985).

Alternatives to Maladaptive Anger
The aim in CBC is not to stop a client from feeling anger, for annoyance or non-demanding anger is a realistic and adaptive response in many situations. However, problems starts when the client exaggerates his frustrations, believing that they are 'awful', and damns the perceived cause of the frustration (for example, the person who thinks, 'She's ruined everything now, damn her!'). The aim in CBC is therefore for the client to experience a degree of annoyance or non-demanding anger appropriate to the situation, by realistically appraising the harm caused to him and by not damning the source of the frustration. The aim is for the client to realistically dislike unpleasant things happening, but not to demand that these things must not happen.

When a person makes a realistic appraisal of harm done to him, he is more likely to analyse the reasons behind what happened and plan how to avoid the frustrations re-occurring. On the other hand, the client who is vigorously damning the cause of the frustration is likely to be more concerned about how to take revenge. Clearly the former approach is the more adaptive and constructive.

Strategies for Working with Clients with Anger Problems

As we have already described, maladaptive anger results when a person demands that a frustration should not have happened, that it is awful that it has happened, and damn the person who caused it to happen. Each of the three components of anger can be dealt with separately. First, it is necessary to challenge the client's idea that bad things must not happen by asking him for the evidence for this belief. Of course, there is no satisfactory evidence for why something must not happen just because we do not want it to happen. Similarly, we may ask the client why other people must follow his personal rules, such as that one must be treated fairly. Again, there is good reason why it is preferable or better for the other person to follow our rule – because the world would be a better place in which to live – but there is no reason why people *must* obey our rules, and it is unrealistic for us to expect so.

An analogy can be usefully employed to illustrate to the client why it is unrealistic to demand that things should happen because we want them to happen. The counsellor can say to the client, 'I must have a million pounds in my hand, right now. I must, I must, I must.' The client can easily see that it is foolish for the counsellor to demand that she must have a million pounds just because she wants it, yet the client is making this very mistake when he demands that other people must behave as he wants them to. Finally, Wessler and Wessler (1980: 98) note that, 'believing, even implicitly, that one can function as a rule-maker for others, for the world, or for nature or God, is grandiose to say the least'.

The second step in dealing with unrealistic anger is to tackle any 'awfulising' about the frustration, where the client is exaggerating the negative consequences of what has happened. The 'What's the evidence?' strategy can again be useful. One thing to note is that it is important to find out the meaning of an event for the angry person, because a seemingly innocuous event may have major significance for the client. Take, for example, a client who is very angry because his wife keeps being late home from work. The significance of the event for the husband might be that the last period when she was frequently late was at a time when she was having an affair, and the husband thinks that this is happening again.

The third part of angry thinking to tackle is the client's damning of the perceived cause of the frustration, be it a person, organisation, circumstances, or the client himself. A key to overcoming this blaming attitude is to help the client to realise that other people *are* fallible and make mistakes, and that just because they may act badly does not mean that they are bad people. This same notion was discussed in Chapter 8, in the context of a depressed person who thinks he is useless or a failure because he fails at things. In the case of depression, the client is not accepting his own fallibility, and in anger it is usually that the client is not accepting the fallibility of others.

In the special case of 'self-defence' anger, described earlier in this chapter, the client is not accepting his own fallibility, and is angry for what he sees as the other person pointing out his unworthiness.

In order to modify the client's damning thinking, a useful approach is to ask the client to justify how the other person can be 'awful' or 'no good' just because he does something that the client does not like. The answers that the client gives are usually to do with his belief that the other person acted badly towards the client or the fact the client does not like the other person's behaviour. However, it does not follow that the other person is therefore bad, worthless or damnable, and the counsellor can point this out to the client.

In the case of self-defence anger, the counsellor would first help the client to modify his self-damning thinking. In self-defence anger, the client believes that to fail at something would mean he was a failure, and it seems to him that the person who is pointing out his failure on a task, is actually saying that he is a failure as a person. The main task of the counsellor is therefore to help the client to realise that he cannot be a failure as a person for failing at a task. The method for achieving this has been described in detail in Chapter 8, in the context of helping the depressed person to modify his negative self-evaluations. The method is similar to that used when challenging the client's damning of other people. Essentially, the counsellor is challenging the logic of the client's thinking, using the 'How does it follow' line of questioning; for example, 'How does it follow that failing on this task shows that you are a failure as a person?'

If the client avoids global negative self-evaluations when he is criticised, he will find it easier to accept just criticisms and respond to unjust criticisms with a more realistic and adaptive level of annoyance. However, the counsellor needs to address the other component of unrealistic thinking in self-defence anger: the client's demanding that other people must not criticise him, and the damning of other people for doing so (for example, 'How dare he speak to me like that. Who does he think he is?') These forms of demanding and damning thinking are similar to those in other sorts of anger, and methods for dealing with them have already been described.

Pitfalls in CBC with Anger Problems

A counsellor will find that it is relatively easy to confront a client with the fact that he has unrealistically demanding expectations of himself. However, she may find it harder to confront the client with the fact that he has unrealistically demanding expectations of other people. The message that one is too hard on oneself is often more palatable than learning that one's attitude to other people is unfair and unreasonable. Bearing this in mind, it is important for the counsellor not to shy away from showing the client that his demands on other people are unrealistic. One strategy which can be helpful is to show the client how he applies an unrealistic personal rule to himself and then to show how he also applies this rule to others. For example, one client with an anger problem was a supervisor in a factory, and she had a harsh attitude towards her staff making mistakes. However, she also applied this perfectionist standard to herself, and the counsellor first showed her how she was unfair to herself in applying the perfectionist standard. When she had accepted this notion, the counsellor showed her how she applied this same rule in an equally unfair way to other people.

One block to changing a client's anger is that anger can often have short-term advantages for the client. For example, a person who is aggressive in a work situation may find that he gets what he wants initially. However, what is the cost? The person's aggressive style is likely to lead to a deterioration in relationships with other people, which will have negative consequences in the long term. Alternatively, a client may enjoy a feeling of power and control over others when he is angry, which he would lose if he learned to control his anger. Some clients also believe that if they do not dominate other people, other people will dominate them. In order to tease out and tackle these blocks to dealing with the anger problem, it is useful to get the client to list the potential advantages and disadvantages of giving up the anger problem. The counsellor can then introduce the idea of short-term advantages versus long-term disadvantages, and deal with any misconceptions the client may have about becoming less angry.

Assertiveness

How a client expresses (or fails to express) his anger, will partly depend on how extreme his angry thinking is, but it will also be determined by the person's skills in communicating anger, and his fears about doing this. There is therefore a clear role for training in assertiveness skills as part of cognitive-behavioural counselling.

Assertiveness is the art of communicating one's opinions, beliefs, feelings and wants in a direct, honest and non-aggressive way (Lange and Jakubowski, 1976). It entails both respecting one's own wishes, and the wishes of other people. A common pattern of unassertiveness is where the unassertive client bottles up his anger and resentment without expressing it, and then blows up in an aggressive way, feels guilty about being so aggressive and then returns back to being submissive. For example, one mother built up a strong resentment about her daughter's untidiness and inconsiderate behaviour, yet she rarely showed this, except for the occasional sarcastic comment. Then, one day they had a huge row, and the mother told her daughter to leave home, which she did. Later, the mother felt guilty about what she had done and asked her daughter to come back home again (which again she did).

The assertive person is neither submissive nor aggressive; he is able to express his likes and dislikes directly and clearly, but in a non-demanding and constructive way. Moreover, whereas the intention of the aggressive person is to harm the other person, the intention of the assertive person is to get what he wants, while respecting the wants of others (Wessler and Wessler, 1980).

These notions can be summed up succinctly using a phrase which is the title of a book on transactional analysis by Harris (1973), *I'm OK, You're OK*:

The aggressive person is saying, 'I'm OK, you're not OK' (what I want is all-important, what you want does not matter).
The submissive person is saying, 'I'm not OK, you're OK' (what I want does not matter, what you want is all-important).
And the assertive person is saying, 'I'm OK, you're OK' (my wishes are important, but I respect yours too).

Blocks to Assertiveness
There are three main cognitive blocks to assertiveness. The first we have already described where a person has a style of thinking where he is damning other people for frustrating him. When a person is preoccupied by thinking how awful other people are for frustrating him, his interactions with other people will be focused on hurting them back, rather than on getting what he wants. Thus, when a person interacts with other people in this frame of mind, his interactions are likely to be aggressive. This sort of damning attitude leads to criticisms which 'put down' the other person, such as 'You are the laziest person I've ever met' or 'You really are useless'.

The second, and perhaps most common block to behaving assertively, is where a person avoids expressing himself for fear of rejection or disapproval. Often the client will describe this in terms of not wanting to 'upset' the other person or make him angry. For example, one client wanted to ask his father to pay more attention to his grandchildren when he came to visit. The client was blocked by the fear that his father would get angry. Another client wanted to ask her husband to spend more time with her, but feared that he would reject her. The unassertive person's fear is based upon evaluations such as 'I must have that other person's approval. If he rejects me, that is awful.' The client may draw the further conclusion that if he is rejected, this must be something to do with him as a person, and he may view the rejection as evidence that he is worthless.

A third main block to assertiveness is where a person feels guilty about acting in a self-interested way and believes it is wrong to try to fulfil his own wishes. This may be because the person has come to believe that self-interested behaviour is selfishness, and that this is wrong. Alternatively, the person may have a low opinion of himself and believe that he does not deserve to get what he wants.

Another way of viewing this same block to assertiveness is that these clients lack a conviction that they have personal rights to speak up for themselves. They are not able to distinguish between healthy self-interest and a total disregard of the needs and wishes of other people. In rational-emotive therapy, there is an explicit notion that acting according to moral codes and protecting the rights of others is a rational and emotionally healthy philosophy to adopt, because this will help to create the sort of society in which we would all like to live (Ellis and Bernard, 1985). At the same time, the excessive self-sacrifice and self-debasement often seen in clients is seen as unhealthy. A significant part of assertiveness training is therefore to do with teaching the client to identify his personal rights for self-expression and self-interested behaviour.

An example of a client whose assertiveness was blocked by guilt was a client who lived in the same village as her mother and who passed her mother's house on the way to the shops each day. The mother wanted to see her daughter every day, although she was often rude to her daughter when she did come. If the daughter did not visit, the mother would keep complaining that the daughter did not care about her (a guilt-inducing strategy). The daughter felt guilty about not wanting to see her mother so frequently because, deep down, she agreed with her mother's comments that she was a bad person for 'neglecting' her mother.

Steps in Assertiveness Training
There are three main steps in assertiveness training (1) discriminating between unassertiveness (submissiveness), assertiveness and aggressiveness. This step also involves teaching the client to be more aware of his personal rights; (2) dealing with the person's cognitive blocks to assertiveness, as described above; (3) behavioural rehearsal of assertiveness in problematic situations by means of role plays and *in vivo* homework tasks. Assertiveness training does not usually proceed through these steps in a neat way, but these are the main components of assertiveness training.

There are also a number of specific techniques which can be taught to clients, and these and other methods are described in more detail in assertiveness manuals such as those by Lange and Jakubowski (1976), Alberti and Emmons (1982), Smith (1975) and Dickson (1982). For example, in many instances where a client wants to express annoyance about something, the following can be a useful formula:

I feel ... ('annoyed')
because ... ('you are late again')
so would you please ... ('telephone me next time if you are going
    to be late').

A typical assertiveness training course might include training in the following assertiveness skills:

making requests (saying what you would like);
refusing requests (saying 'no');
expressing non-damning anger or annoyance;
dealing with criticism;
expressing and receiving compliments/appreciation;
expressing and receiving apologies.

One can see from this list that assertiveness does not just concern confrontation with other people, but also includes skills such as how to show appreciation to other people. Often this is as hard for people to do as expressing negative feelings.

We have ended this chapter with the topic of assertiveness because it involves using CBC to tackle a number of different emotional problems. Assertiveness training may, for example, involve helping a client to overcome anxiety about expressing annoyance, guilt about saying 'no', embarrassment about expressing a compliment, and to control anger. Moreover, assertiveness helps a client to feel more in control of his life, and provides a healthy antidote to depression resulting from helplessness and hopelessness.

Cognitive-behavioural counselling provides a comprehensive and effective approach to many emotional problems. However, many of the methods described are much easier to understand than they are to employ, and there are many blocks to client progress. Notwithstanding these difficulties, we hope that readers will find this book to be useful and will persevere in learning the methods of cognitive-behavioural counselling.

References

Alberti, R.E. and Emmons, M.E. (1982) *Your Perfect Right*, 4th edition. San Luis Obispo, CA: Impact.

American Psychiatric Association (1987) *Diagnostic and Statistical Manual of Mental Disorder – III (Revised)*. Washington: American Psychiatric Press.

Amies, P.L., Gelder, M.G., and Shaw, P.M. (1983) 'Social Phobia: A Comparative Clinical Study', *British Journal of Psychiatry*, 142: 174–9.

Argyle, M. and Trower, P. (1979) *Person to Person*. London: Harper & Row.

Beck A.T. (1970) 'The Core Problems in Depression: The Cognitive Triad', in J. Masserman (ed.), *Depression: Theories and Therapies*. New York: Grune & Stratton.

Beck, A.T. (1976) *Cognitive Therapy and the Emotional Disorders*. New York: New American Library.

Beck, A.T. (1985) 'Theoretical and Clinical Aspects', in A.T. Beck and G. Emery, *Anxiety Disorders and Phobias: A Cognitive Perspective*. New York: Basic Books.

Beck, A.T., Rush, A.J., Shaw, B.F., and Emery, G. (1979) *Cognitive Therapy of Depression*. New York: Guilford Press.

Blackburn, I. (1987) *Coping with Depression*. Edinburgh: Chambers.

Burns, D.D. (1980) *Feeling Good: The New Mood Therapy*. New York: William Morrow.

Chesney, M.A., and Rosenman, R.H. (eds) (1985) *Anger and Hostility in Cardiovascular and Behavioral Disorders*. Washington: Hemisphere.

Clark, D.M., Salkovskis, P.M., and Chalkley, A.J. (1985) 'Respiratory Control Treatment for Panic Attacks', *Journal of Behavior Therapy and Experimental Psychiatry*, 16 (1): 23–30.

Costello, C.G. (1972) 'Depression: Loss of Reinforcers or Loss of Reinforcer Effectiveness', *Behavior Therapy*, 3: 240–7.

Duck, S.W., and Gilmour, R. (eds) (1981) *Personal Relationships*, Volume 1: *Studying Personal Relationships*. London and New York: Academic Press.

Dickson, A. (1982) *A Woman in Your Own Right*. London: Quartet.

Dryden, W. (1984) *Rational-Emotive Therapy: Fundamentals and Innovations*. Beckenham, Kent: Croom Helm.

Dryden, W. (1987) *Counselling Individuals: The Rational-Emotive Approach*. London: Taylor & Francis.

Edelmann, R.J. (1987) *The Psychology of Embarrassment*. Chichester, Sussex: Wiley.

Ellis, A. (1962) *Reason and Emotion in Psychotherapy*. New York: Lyle Stuart.

Ellis, A. (1977) 'The Basic Clinical Theory of Rational-Emotive Therapy', in A. Ellis and R. Grieger (eds), *Handbook of Rational-Emotive Therapy*. New York: Springer.

Ellis, A. (1979) 'The Theory of Rational-Emotive Therapy', in A. Ellis and J.M. Whiteley (eds), *Theoretical and Empirical Foundations of Rational-Emotive Therapy*. Monterey, CA: Brooks/Cole.

Ellis, A. and Bernard, M.E. (1985) 'What is Rational-Emotive Therapy (RET)?', in A. Ellis and M.E. Bernard (eds), *Clinical Applications of Rational-Emotive Therapy*. New York: Plenum.

Ellis, A. and Dryden, W. (1987) *The Practice of Rational-Emotive Therapy*. New York: Springer.

Ellis, A. and Harper, R.A. (1975) *A New Guide to Rational Living*. Hollywood, CA: Wilshire Books.

Emery, G. (1982) *Own Your Own Life*. New York: Signet.

Emery, G. (1985) 'Cognitive Therapy: Techniques and Applications', in A.T. Beck and G. Emery, *Anxiety Disorders and Phobias: A Cognitive Perspective*. New York: Basic Books.

Festinger, L. (1957) *A Theory of Cognitive Dissonance*. Stanford, CA: Stanford University Press.

Frank, J.D. (1961) *Persuasion and Healing*. Baltimore, MD: Johns Hopkins University.

Gilbert, P. (1986) 'Cognitive Therapy Training Tape'. Unpublished training videotape, South Derbyshire District Health Authority.

Goffman, E. (1971) *Relations in Public*. Harmondsworth, Mddx: Allen Lane/ Penguin.

Harris, T.A. (1973) *I'm O.K., You're O.K.* London: Pan.

Hauck, P. (1974) *Calm Down: How to Cope with Frustration and Anger*. Philadelphia, PA: Westminster Press.

Jacobsen, E. (1938) *Progressive Relaxation*. Chicago: University of Chicago.

Kanfer, F.H. and Goldstein, A.P. (eds) (1980) *Helping People Change*, 2nd edition. New York: Pergamon.

Kelly, G. (1955) *The Psychology of Personal Constructs*. New York: W.W. Norton.

Lange, A. and Jakubowski, P. (1976) *Responsible Assertive Behavior: Cognitive-Behavioral Procedures for Trainers*. Champaign, IL: Research Press.

Lazarus, A.A. (1981) *The Practice of Multimodal Therapy*. New York: McGraw Hill.

Lazarus, R.S. (1966) *Psychological Stress and the Coping Process*. New York: McGraw Hill.

Lembo, J.M. (1977) *How to Cope with Your Fears and Frustrations*. New York: Libra.

Meichenbaum, D. (1985) *Stress Inoculation Training*. New York: Pergamon.

Maultsby, M.C. (1975) *Help Yourself to Happiness*. New York: Institute for Rational Living.

Smith, M. (1975) *When I Say No, I Feel Guilty*. New York: Dial.

Spivack, G., Platt, J.J., and Shure, M.B. (1976) *The Problem-Solving Approach to Adjustment*. San Francisco: Jossey Bass.

Storr, A. (1979) *The Art of Psychotherapy*. London: Secker & Warburg.

Trower, P., Bryant, B., and Argyle, M. (1978) *Social Skills and Mental Health*. London: Methuen.

Trower, P. and Turland, D. (1984) 'Social Phobia', in S.M. Turner (ed.), *Behavioral Theories and Treatment of Anxiety*. New York: Plenum.

Wessler, R.A. and Wessler, R.L. (1980) *The Principles and Practice of Rational-Emotive Therapy*. San Francisco: Jossey-Bass.

Wolpe, J. (1958) *Psychotherapy by Reciprocal Inhibition*. Stanford, CA: Stanford University Press.

Index

ABC assessment form, 23, 24–5, 26, 32–3, 78, 79, 98–100, 102
ABC model, 3–4, 21–9, 42–55; As, 47–9; Bs, 49–55; Cs, 43–7; negotiating with client, 30–1
abortion, 137, 140
absolutistic/dichotomous thinking, 52, 54–5, 65–6, 110
achievement ratings, 126–7
activating events, 3, 32, 47–9, 56, 67, 93–4
activity planning, 124–6
agenda setting, 37, 40, 72
agoraphobia, 6, 111, 118
analogies, 89, 127
anger, 45, 138, 140–5
anxiety, 45, 107, 109–21; behavioural aspects, 118–19; cognitive aspects, 115–18; somatic aspects, 119–21; types, 111–15; see also social anxiety
apathy, 124
appraisal of events, 42–3, 109, 112, 142
assertiveness, 138, 145–8; training, 95, 147–8
assessment of problem, 18–21; ABC, 22–5, 26–7, 28–9, 42–3; sharing with client, 27–9
attention-seeking, 132, 133
'automatic thoughts', 2, 4
avoidance behaviour, 45, 107, 109, 111, 112, 118

Beck, A., 2, 4, 68, 91, 109, 110, 122, 126, 131
behavioural counselling, 6, 21, 37, 44–5
behavioural tasks, 93, 102–5
beliefs, 21–2, 56–7, 67–8; and emotional insight, 76–81; and real-life exposure, 81–2; core, 26, 75–6; irrational, 1–2, 3, 26; testing, 5, 102–3, 106–7, 128; types, 50–5; see also disputing; evaluations; inferences
biographical data sheet, 14, 16
blocks to change, overcoming, 71–2, 73–83
bodily sensations, 44, 46–7, 109, 111, 119–21
boundary conditions, negotiating, 36–7
breathing problems, 111, 119–20

chaining, 56; and disputing, 67–8, 78
change: assessing, 92, 101; emotional/behavioural, 78–9, 91–2, 96, 128; of

circumstances, 32, 93–6; of values, 139–40; overcoming blocks to, 71–2, 73–83
childhood experiences, 7–8
collaboration, principle of, 37
confidence: counsellor's, 15; loss of, 112, 114
contract, therapeutic, 37
criticism, see evaluations; rejection

damning, 139, 140, 142, 143–4, 146
demands v. preferences, 55, 66, 89, 143, 144
dependency beliefs, 71, 72, 83–4
depression, 4, 45, 51, 60, 76–9, 80, 94, 103–4, 122–34
disputing negative thinking, 5, 59–68, 78, 81, 83–4, 88–91, 93, 100–3, 104, 116–17, 129–31, 139–40, 143–4; checklist for, 101–2
distraction, 92–3
Dryden, W., 64, 74, 93, 135–6, 137–8, 141

Ellis, A., 2–3, 64, 68, 91, 107
embarrassment, 135–6, 137
emotional episodes, 22, 75, 77–9, 93, 98, 100
emotional insight, 76–81
evaluations, 3, 43, 50, 53–5, 57, 58, 110, 116; by others, 3, 4, 5, 63–4, 89, 113, 137, 141, 144, 146; disputing, 61–7, 129–31, 139–40, 143–4; global, 54, 64–5, 129–31, 139, 144; self-, 54, 55, 63, 105, 129–31, 135; types, 54, 63–4
exaggeration, 52, 64–5
expectations of client, initial, 13, 15–16, 17, 18

'failure', 129–30
fear, 115–17; see also panic; phobias
feedback from client, 40, 73, 133
feelings: causation, 1, 3, 24; changing, 78–9, 91–2, 128; inductions/re-experiencing, 77–9; intensity, 44; types, 44; see also emotional episodes
formulation of problem, 26–7, 75–6
frustration, 140, 142, 143

goals of therapy, negotiating, 31–4
graded exposure, 118–19
guilt, 100, 123, 137–40, 147

Index compiled by Peva Keane